Mary Catherine Crowley

An Every Day Girl

Mary Catherine Crowley

An Every Day Girl

ISBN/EAN: 9783742833037

Manufactured in Europe, USA, Canada, Australia, Japa

Cover: Foto ©Thomas Meinert / pixelio.de

Manufactured and distributed by brebook publishing software (www.brebook.com)

Mary Catherine Crowley

An Every Day Girl

"THE FRIGHTENED ANIMAL PLUNGED INTO THE ROOM."
(See page 56.)

AN EVERY-DAY GIRL.

BY

MARY CATHERINE CROWLEY,

Author of "Merry Hearts and True," "Happy-Go-Lucky,"
"Apples Ripe and Rosy," "The City of Wonders,"
"Short Stories," etc.

NEW YORK, CINCINNATI, CHICAGO:
BENZIGER BROTHERS,

Copyright, 1930, by BENZIGER BROTHERS

Printed in the United States of America

CONTENTS.

	PAGE
CHAPTER I.	
AN AWAKENING...............................	7
CHAPTER II.	
TESSIE IN CHARGE............................	16
CHAPTER III.	
A TELEGRAM AND A VISITOR...................	28
CHAPTER IV.	
THE COOKING CLASS.	39
CHAPTER V.	
TWO YOUNG HOSTESSES........................	48
CHAPTER VI.	
MISS LANGDON'S SCHOOL......................	60
CHAPTER VII.	
MARY RENWICK...............................	70

CHAPTER VIII.
Mother's Welcome Home...................... 85

CHAPTER IX.
Signorina and Princess....................... 96

CHAPTER X.
An Aboriginal Celebration................... 108

CHAPTER XI.
The Literary Club........................... 118

CHAPTER XII.
The Growth of the Brambles................. 134

CHAPTER XIII.
The Queen's Lace Handkerchief.............. 145

CHAPTER XIV.
An Indian Sphinx............................ 156

CHAPTER XV.
Miss Langdon Explains the Mystery......... 169

CHAPTER XVI.
A Choice of Heroines........................ 178

AN EVERY-DAY GIRL.

CHAPTER I.

AN AWAKENING.

"Of course you will go," said Mr. Marron, as his wife finished reading aloud a letter received by the afternoon mail.

"Oh, dear, no!—how can I?" and, with a light laugh, the lady glanced towards the group of children gathered around the sitting-room table, and thought of her many home duties.

"What is it, mother?" asked Tessie, her eldest daughter, who entered the room just in time to catch the last words.

"Your Aunt Emily writes that she and father insist upon my paying them a visit in New York. They are to be at the Fifth

Avenue Hotel for the winter, and she wants me to start on Thursday."

Tessie appeared a trifle dazed. Mother to go off by herself for a holiday, and leave all care behind? Such a project had never been heard of within her recollection.

"I shall answer the letter to-night," continued Mrs. Marron, "and remind Emily I am a staid materfamilias, and cannot pack my trunk and start on a tour as independently as she, a spinster of comfortable fortune."

"Why should you do anything of the kind?" objected her husband. "You ought to go; you have not seen your father and sister since their return from Europe—you will meet many of your old friends, too, and, above all, the change will do you good."

The blithe little woman regarded him with astonishment.

"It is out of the question, my dear," she reasoned; "who would keep house, and look after May and Toosie and the boys?"

"Tessie, to be sure. The Christmas vacation is but begun; this is your opportunity."

"The poor child has had no experience; I am afraid she would never get along."

"It is a pretty how d'ye do if a girl of sixteen has not learned to help her mother," Mr. Marron rejoined, taking up his newspaper.

Tessie's cheeks flushed, and her eyes filled with tears. She suddenly realized that if she had been more interested in household matters she might have been of much assistance in many little ways.

"Tessie is a good girl," the considerate mother hastened to say, "but with her studies and music she has no time for other occupations."

"She should be able to make herself useful."

"I might try," ventured Tessie, in a deprecating manner.

"Yes, do try, my daughter," encouraged her father, mollified at once. "We will all endeavor to make it easy for you, and mother shall have her happy holiday."

Mrs. Marron demurred a while longer, but finally, half lest Tessie might be considered remiss in any duty, she yielded to the loving arguments of the family, and an hour later sent a reply to Aunt Emily accepting the invitation.

The Marrons lived in one of the beautiful cities of the interior of New York State. Their home, which stood in the centre of a garden, was an old-fashioned two-storied Dutch structure, built of the brownstone abounding in the vicinity; the façade was covered with white stucco, in the long, sloping roof were quaint dormer casements, and high up at the side of the building were two tiny "windowlets," as Tessie named them, because they measured only ten by eighteen inches. These last gave light to the garret—

perfect museum of curiosities. They looked like a pair of spectacles, and shadowed by the moss-grown eaves suggested a resemblance to an antiquated Holland dame in fantastic head-dress, peering through her glasses at the passers-by.

Below were square sashes with small panes, and wooden shutters once white, but now painted a dark green. Along the front of the house, and giving it a sociable air, extended a vine-covered veranda with a low baluster and broad benches. A bricked walk led, in the straightest of straight lines, up the distance of a few rods from the gate to the single step of this veranda. Crossing the latter, the visitor stood before a green door ornamented by a brass knocker—the grotesque head of an animal " never seen on sea or land." It was a curious door, divided horizontally, and in spring or summer the upper half was always open, affording from without a glimpse of a low studded hall, and the pleasant parlor on the right or the sitting-room to the left, with their wide chimney caverns filled in perhaps with branches of apple-blossoms, or that shrub of furzy, feathery bloom aptly known as the " smoke-tree."

"A shabby old house," Tessie often pronounced it, as compared with the more modern residences of her friends. She did not appreciate its picturesque charm, and could not understand why an artist once asked permission to sketch it, nor why, one morning, a tourist party of amateur photographers pointed their cameras at it from every quarter, like so many cannon directed towards an ancient fort.

But mother was going away, and what an excitement there was in helping on her preparations!

"Dear me, mother!" declared the young girl, as she attempted to lend her aid with the packing, "I am afraid Aunt Emily will think you are not a bit stylish. Why don't you have pretty gowns and wraps like other girls' mothers? This season, for instance, Mrs. Gaines wears a handsome black silk gown half covered with jet, a natty sealskin jacket, and a little round hat. Her hair is curled in short, soft rings about her face, and she looks so young one would never suppose she had a tall daughter like Laura. I am sure she would always be ready, as far as her wardrobe is concerned, for a trip to the ends of the earth. Why did not you get a black silk? Father wanted you to have it, but you do not seem to care for such things at all."

Mrs. Marron smiled a trifle wistfully. She did not consider it necessary to explain that the money intended for the rich gown went to pay the music-teacher, and for the painting-lessons Tessie was so anxious to have because several of her friends belonged to the class. Yet perhaps a suspicion approaching the truth flashed upon the young girl, as she took from a bandbox her mother's bonnet, home-made and tasteful, but lacking in the illusive quality termed *chic*, so seldom bestowed save by the trained milliner. For the first time she was struck by the difference between it and her own modish hat trimmed with ostrich plumes, bought at the most fashionable establishment in town.

"Mother dear," she said softly, "you always sacrifice yourself for us. How selfish I have been not to see that you buy the pretty things for me and for the little girls, instead of for yourself."

"Nonsense!" returned Mrs. Marron, "I have good children and all I need besides;" but she looked pleased at the evidence of appreciation.

When the appointed day arrived, and the beloved traveller came down-stairs ready for the journey, Tessie, despite her previous criticism, concluded that her mother made a better appearance than Mrs. Gaines, after all. For her simple costume was exquisitely neat, and although the most retiring of women, Mrs. Marron was distinguished by the indescribable air of refinement that comes of gentle thoughts as well as gentle manners, and which fashionable attire alone can never give.

What affectionate leave-takings there were in the hall! May and Toosie clung to her until the last minute; Joe and Ben were solemn and glum. They had anticipated "jolly larks" during her absence, but now when she was actually about to start the prospect did not seem so pleasant, and they wondered rather dolefully "what home would be like without mother."

"Good-by," she said. "Write to me, boys, and do not get into mischief. Little girls, you will try to be good, I am sure. Be careful they do not take cold, Tessie. Good-by, my daughter. Keep a brave heart and remember you are being a real help to me." The next moment Mr. Marron handed her into the carriage waiting at the gate, stepped in after her, and presently it rolled away amid a waving of handkerchiefs and followed by farewell cheers from the boys, a piping echo from May, and a wail from little Toosie.

Tessie folded her lips tightly together and determined not to give way in the least bit to loneliness, because "mamma would not like it." With a soothing word she drew Toosie into the house, May following close. Shutting the door, she seated herself upon the cosy sofa in the hall, and drawing them down beside her among its pillows told them a wonderful fairy story. Toosie's spirits rose like a toy balloon, May listened with shining eyes, and at the conclusion the two children ran away laughing merrily to tease Delia, the cook, for ginger-cakes, and feast with the dolls in the play room. The boys had promptly betaken themselves to the wood-shed, where they were engaged in some mysterious carpentering.

"Delia is my consolation!" soliloquized Tessie, as she heard the good woman's cheery voice repeating: "Cookies, is it? Sure, me darlin's, in coorse ye shall have them." Another time she might have said, "Be off with yez! Don't be askin' me to stop in me work," and they would scamper away, coming back almost immediately to find a small pile of cookies lying as if by accident upon a corner of the kitchen table, while Delia, busier than ever, rattled away at the dishes in the pantry, "putting the shelves to rights."

But this was an extraordinary occasion. "Poor dears, they miss their mother," she reflected: and ginger-cakes having always proved a solace for their childish griefs, she gave them three in each hand now, and filled the little pockets of their frocks besides.

Delia was that *rara avis* among domestic auxiliaries, "a treasure." She had lived with the Marrons ever since Tessie was a baby and everybody agreed "they thought the world of her." It was furthermore hinted she could never get along anywhere else, since she did not like interference in her special domain, was not slow in expressing her mind if anything displeased her, and sometimes volunteered advice in household matters. The younger members of the family managed to steer clear of Delia's peculiarities, however, and Mrs. Marron had a way of quietly overruling her whims and humors when necessary, while remembering there were to be weighed against them years of faithful service and a devotedness that had never failed.

CHAPTER II.

TESSIE IN CHARGE.

MRS. MARRON would not have decided upon the visit to New York but for her confidence in Delia. She knew this faithful domestic helper would keep the household machinery running smoothly; Tessie's principal obligation would be to look after the two small children a little, and try to keep the boys out of "scrapes"; to be ready with a smiling face for breakfast with her father in the morning, and to welcome him when he came home from his counting-room at noon, and after the cares of the day.

"I shall say a prayer every morning that I may be faithful to every duty which presents itself," the young girl resolved in the quiet of her own room the evening after her mother's departure; then, looking up at a favorite picture of the dear Madonna of the little home of Nazareth, she added softly: "I will strive to be gentle, self-forgetful, and loving, as She was."

For nearly a week everything went beautifully. The boys were remarkably well-behaved. One of their Christmas presents had been a miniature stationary engine, that could get up real steam and go "like thunder," Ben averred. Naturally much of their time was spent in experimenting with it. May and Toosie were as docile and sweet as possible. Tessie could always insure their obedience by the promise of a story. Delia made all comfortable, dinner was never late, Tessie was always pleasant. Her father said she was fast becoming a model housekeeper and the letters to her mother contained only encouraging news.

"Have a good time, and do not feel obliged to hurry home," wrote Tessie.

"Our eldest daughter is managing splendidly," proudly reported Mr. Marron.

Laura Gaines had spent Christmas with relatives in Albany. The very day she reached home she went over to the Marrons'. Tessie, catching a glimpse of her from the window, ran to the door to admit her, and after a gay greeting led her into the sitting-room.

For a while the two friends chatted volubly, both talking at once, yet each keeping the thread of the other's narrative in the marvellous manner of schoolgirls. At length Laura asked:

"How do you get along without your mother? How do you ever manage the *ménage?*" Laura affected French words and phrases under the mistaken notion that they imparted an elegance to her conversation.

"Oh, we miss mother, of course," replied Tessie. "But it is the easiest matter in the world to keep house. I cannot understand what some people consider so difficult about it. Delia gives the orders to the marketman, who calls regularly, and everything goes on as serenely as possible. Yes, sometimes the care seems to wear upon mother, but I do not mind it at all. Indeed, the reality is much like 'playing house,' as we used to do years ago; do not you remember when an empty packing-case in the garret was our palatial dwelling, and we served sumptuous repasts of sugar-plums and peanuts upon a table made of a soap-box turned upside down?"

They laughed over the recollection, but Laura was duly impressed.

"Tessie Marron is the smartest girl I know," she announced later to a number of their mutual friends. "She is keeping house, and does not find it a bit of trouble. I could never do it, now could you?"

Several of the girls shrugged their shoulders. They evidently thought themselves quite as clever as Tessie, and able to acquit themselves as creditably in this respect as in all others. Nevertheless, Tessie's ability had actually been put to the test, and, although they would not have admitted the fact, they began to regard her as entitled to consideration: since she was enjoying a wider experience than themselves, and from all accounts knew how to manage as well, if not better, than her mother.

But all this was too Utopian to last. One morning Toosie awoke fretful and cross, Tessie lost patience with her, and came flurried and late to breakfast. The boys were behind time also, and when they appeared they were inopportunely in a glee and refused to be suppressed. Mr. Marron, who was abstracted, and annoyed about business matters, spoke to them once or twice. Tessie unwisely tried to make excuses for them in a manner that appeared to him pert, and he sharply reproved her.

"O dear! everything is going wrong to-day," she said to herself, swallowing a queer lump in her throat.

When her father had gone she bustled about for half-an-hour, flourishing a rose-colored dusting-cloth, and creating a general semblance of order. May and Toosie (the latter was not yet grown up to her real name, Jessica) were amusing themselves in the play-room. The boys had gone out.

"Now," soliloquized the older sister, "I will betake myself to the sitting-room, and finish that lovely story I began to read yesterday."

An hour passed. Ensconced in her mother's sewing-chair, Tessie rocked and read, refreshing herself now and again with candy she had made the day before. The winter sunshine flooded the room, the plants on the broad window ledge wore a brighter green; outside, the sparrows hopped to and fro on the frozen lawn as gayly as though it were verdant, velvety turf; within, the fire of hickory logs on the hearth crackled now and again, and burst into a new flame. Tessie's late vexations were forgotten.

Suddenly there was a sound of some commotion in the garden at the rear of the house, and presently Joe's voice called from the hall: "Tessie, where are you? Come, quick! Ben has fallen out of a tree and is 'most killed; he's dead, sure!"

Tessie's heart seemed to give a bound, and then to stand still. She was too frightened to notice the contradictory nature of the intelligence. Instinctively echoing the fervent cry of "God help us" with which Delia had already rushed out from the kitchen, she followed mechanically. Prone upon the ground under the cherry tree was Ben, apparently lifeless.

The frightened girl stood looking on in a bewildered way, while Delia gathered him up in her strong arms, carried him to the house, and gently laid him on the sofa in the sitting-room.

"Whisht, alanna, don't cry!" whispered the resourceful woman; "I doubt if it is really sinseless he is—only a bit bewildered like, and a good bit scared. Fetch cold water and open the windows so as to give him air. Don't crowd around him, children; you, Joe, quit endeavoring to get him to speak and be off for Dr. Shaw as fast as you can."

Joe needed no second bidding, but vanished precipitately.

"Run away to the play room, little ones," said Tessie peremptorily.

May and Toosie went unwillingly and in high dudgeon; they were too alarmed to disobey. Then Tessie, having brought the water, stood by helplessly, while Delia sprinkled some of it on Ben's face and bathed his head. This treatment and the fresh air blowing in at the window soon revived him. By the time the doctor arrived he was sitting bolt upright on the sofa, feeling of his arms and legs "to make sure they were all there," he explained.

"You have done just what was best," said Dr. Shaw, turning to the anxious attendants after a careful examination of the patient. "Ben, you rogue, do not try any such ground and lofty tumbling again. But you are all right, I think.

"The result might indeed have been serious," he said to Delia, who accompanied him to the door, "but by a happy providence the boy, as far as can be judged at present, has suffered no injury to the brain, and he has also escaped without any broken bones. Keep a special eye on him for a few days, however, and send for me if he appears in any way different from usual."

"A special eye!" repeated Delia to herself, as she returned to the room; "and the other eye must be upon the cherubs, as their father jestingly calls the two little girls. Sure, I'd need a hundred eyes to keep track of all the pranks of these children—blessings on them all the same, though they do pester me, and no mistake!"

As Ben evinced no symptoms but those of plotting mischief, which were assuredly not unusual, Tessie, overjoyed as she was at his preservation, gave way after a while to her overwrought emotions:

"Well, Ben Marron!" she began. "What did you expect to find up a cherry tree this time of the year? Neither fruit nor birds' eggs, certainly; even the squirrels that emigrated there when the old hickory tree was cut down have been hunted out long ago."

"Oh," interposed Joe, who, as his brother was kept indoors, loitered around the house all the afternoon, "we were climbing for practise. I dared Ben to go out on a little limb near the top of the tree, and he did. The limb was dead, you see, though we did not know it, and he came down plumperty-plump! He ought not to have taken the dare, you know."

"It is you who ought not to have dared a fellow," growled Ben, looking as though he would like to argue the question with his fists.

"Stop, both of you! No one must say another word about it," directed his sister, with an assumption of authority, at which the boys exchanged a glance of amused protest that immediately effected a reconciliation between them.

* * * *

A few days after this escapade had created such alarm in the Marron household, the town awoke one morning to find the ground covered with snow, the first of the New Year. The boys and the two little girls were jubilant.

"It came just because we wanted it!" cried Toosie, with childish self-conceit.

By midday the sun shone forth through the clouds, and early in the afternoon the two little children were trotting around the garden, laughing at their footprints in the snow and, in their pretty gray and red coats, reminding Tessie of a pair of belated robins as they flitted hither and thither.

It was hard work dragging their sleds, however; they grew tired, and with a tacit agreement that they would go stand at the front gate and watch the passers-by (their usual occupation when waiting for some other diversion to turn up), they went around the corner of the house. Here an unexpected source of pleasure awaited them. From the roof of the veranda the fast-melting snow dripped in a steady rain.

"Let us stay here and catch the bright drops as they come down," exclaimed May.

"Oh, yes, it will be great sport," agreed Toosie.

So the two stood under the shower, holding out their chubby hands for the sunlit drops that were beautiful as jewels.

"It is like acting out one of Tessie's fairy stories," May declared. "Here are diamonds and pearls falling, falling all the time, only they slip through our fingers so we are never able to keep any."

Blithe little May had yet to learn the difference between fairyland and reality. In real life we have to work for our treasures; if we merely stand and wait for them, catching at everything that gleams before us, it will be to find our hands empty in the end.

But the roof continued to send down this illusive wealth upon them, embroidering with sparkling gems the gay coats and rakish hoods in prodigal profusion. Tessie, skimming through another fascinating story, heard the children's shouts of merriment. "How happy they are!" she murmured, without looking up from her book.

Yet even holding out their hands for jewels to fall into them became monotonous after a while to these restless small folk.

"Play I was a steam-car, and I came along and ran over you," suggested May, casting about for a new game.

"No!" objected Toosie. "Play I was a whale, and came right up out of this puddle and swallowed you."

"The steam-car is better," persisted the older midget, running up against her small sister with some force.

To Toosie's ready fancy May's sturdy little figure, and round, rosy face, suddenly assumed the gigantic proportions of a great, black, snorting monster, menacing her with destruction.

"Oh, my!" she shrieked, with a ridiculous but unfeigned fear. "I am run over, I am run over! Oh—oo—oh—oo!"

May paused in indecision. Then the thought of how terrible it would be if Toosie were indeed run over by a train presented itself with all the vividness of an actual occurrence. In an absurd fright at being, as she imagined, the cause of this dire calamity, she forthwith screamed, too, with all her might:

"Ow, ow! Toosie is run over, and I did it, 'cause I was a steam-car; but I couldn't help it, for the big whale was going to eat me up! Ow, ow!"

Their cries rose to the windows of Tessie's room, and in a flutter of anxiety she rushed down the stairs and out of the house. There, under the eaves of the veranda, stood the two little girls, their dainty coats and hoods drenched with snow-water, their fingers and noses blue with cold, and the tears running down their cheeks while they continued to clamor vigorously, growing every moment more and more frightened by the bugaboos they had conjured up.

"Hush, hush! What is the matter? You will alarm the neighborhood," admonished the young girl, looking around to see whence danger threatened them.

"I've been run over by a terrible steam-car!" bemoaned Toosie.

"And I've been swallowed by a frightful big whale," sobbed May.

Tessie received this ludicrous explanation with a peal of merriment, and so reassuring was the sound that they forgot to be vexed with her for laughing at them.

"You dreadful children!" she remonstrated at last, realizing their bedraggled condition. "Come right into the house and get off those soaking wet coats and hoods."

That night she was awakened by a queer sound almost like the barking of a dog, which proceeded from the room where the two little girls slept. It was Toosie coughing and crying with an attack of croup, and May was found to have taken a severe influenza.

The first thing to be done was to summon Delia; the next, to arouse father and ask him to go for the doctor. After what seemed an interminable delay, but was in fact only a short time, Dr. Shaw again arrived. Delia had been active in the interval, and when he had administered the remedies he had brought with him he said, turning to her:

"Now swathe these pappooses in hot blankets like genuine Indian babies; do not worry, Miss Tessie, they are better already; I will call again in the morning."

Delia soon transformed the culprits into two queer little bundles with only their eyes and noses visible, and before long the strange barking ceased, and both Toosie and May dozed off into the peaceful sleep which appertains to small folk poetically supposed to be endowed with the nature of cherubs.

CHAPTER III.

A TELEGRAM AND A VISITOR.

AFTER a few days the cherubs had quite recovered from the effects of the singular railway collision and the menaces of the imaginary whale; and Ben's wits, as Joe claimed, far from suffering injury, had been simply shaken up by his fall from the cherry tree.

Tessie earnestly hoped the routine of home life would be broken by no other exciting incidents before her mother's return; she began to understand why mamma always included among the intentions of the daily rosary "that the children might be preserved from all physical as well as spiritual danger."

The next sensation was a telegram for Delia.

At sight of the yellow envelope the good woman looked as alarmed as though confronted by an apparition. "Do *you* open it, Miss Tessie," she begged, refusing to touch it herself, and excitedly wringing her hands. "Wirrasthrue! My sister in Syracuse or one of the childer must be dead, no less! Oh, that I should live to see the day!"

They were still in the hall, whither she had been summoned by the door-bell, and sitting down on the stairs she put her apron to her eyes and began to weep bitterly. Joe, who stood by, sniffed sympathetically, and May and Toosie, having just appeared upon the scene, were on the point of setting up a wail of their own as soon as they perceived the distress of the friend who always took their part when they were in trouble.

"Don't, Delia, don't take on so—at least until you hear what the news is!" pleaded Tessie, tearing open the message. "Listen, this is what it says: 'The wedding is day after to-morrow; Kate's heart is set on having you here.'"

The figure rocking to and fro in an abandonment of grief stopped abruptly. The good woman was for a second speechless, but her round, shining face looked out from behind the apron like the sun emerging from a cloud.

"Well, did any one ever hear the like!" she broke out at length. "Bad cess to them for putting me in such a tremor! Isn't it enough to fash a saint? What would I want at the wedding? Not but I might have taken a run down for the day if the mistress was at home—Kate being my sister's oldest daughter, and me being her godmother besides. A grand man she's getting, a plumber by trade, and a member of the parish temperance society; but she deserves the best of luck, for she was ever dutiful to her father and mother. Of coorse I'd like to see her married, if so 'twas I could go—but since 'tis not to be thought of, Miss Tessie, dear, you'll write a bit of a note for me, saying I wish the colleen and her choice all happiness, and I send my last month's wages for Kate to buy herself a present according to her taste."

Having obtained a promise that a letter should be written the same evening, Delia betook herself to the kitchen, studying the telegram, which she had at last ventured to take into her own hands.

"Could we not manage to let Delia go, after all?" said Tessie to her father an hour later. "She would only be away twenty-four hours."

"I think we could get along very well during the interval, since you are becoming so proficient a housekeeper, my dear," responded Mr. Marron heartily.

"You won't mind meals served somewhat *à la picnic* for a day?" stipulated his daughter, flushing with pleasure at his praise, but with a little anxious frown, as she remembered that there might be a few hitches in the working of the domestic machinery when she was left to keep it running entirely according to her own devices.

"Not at all; if we choose to have a winter picnic by our own fireside it will be all the merrier, and we will agree beforehand that no grumbling or fault-finding is to be allowed."

"Oh, you *are* the dearest father!" cried Tessie, giving him an affectionate kiss.

"Is it to leave you all, like a brood of orphan chicks, with no one to look after you? Not if every one of my kith and kin was going to be married!" exclaimed Delia, when informed of the proposed arrangement.

"But father is not an orphan chick," answered Tessie, laughing, "and since there is no prospect of weddings being so frequent in your family, we think you ought not to miss this one."

As the faithful creature really longed to go, and was only restrained by a sense of duty, Tessie's arguments, supplemented by Mr. Marron's positive command, triumphed in the end. The second day following she set out for Syracuse, yet not without sundry misgivings and repeated instructions to the young mistress of the house, and after embracing the little girls as fondly as if she were about to depart for the ends of the earth. As the stout figure in the purple merino gown, broché shawl, and bonnet with nodding green plumes disappeared down the street, Tessie's heart sank. A peep into the well-provisioned pantry presently reassured her, however, and there was a certain satisfaction in finding herself in entire charge of the household.

"I'm not going to begin by borrowing trouble, anyhow!" she thought.

But trouble often comes fast enough without being called up by telephone, as one may say. The time allotted for Delia's visit passed uneventfully, and at the hour when she was expected to return all the children were at the front gate waiting for her.

Alas, she did not come! Instead, the telegraph boy appeared once more, but this time the message was from the Syracuse Hospital. It said: "Delia Reardon was run down by a bicyclist when she was hurrying to the train this morning; a sprained ankle; patient suffering also from the shock."

It was now Tessie's turn to sink down upon the stairs with lamenting. Her first thought was not in truth a selfish one.

"Poor, poor Delia!" she ejaculated; "Ben and Joe, carry word to father down-town immediately. He will know what to do."

* * * *

Mr. Marron sent a dispatch to the hospital, directing that the devoted servant who had been so long in his family should receive every attention and care at his expense, and Tessie wrote a sympathetic letter, bidding Delia not to worry, for they were getting on well, and Mrs. Flaherty (a humble friend in need) was to come every day and attend to the work of the house.

The young girl wrote more bravely than she felt, however. "Misfortunes seldom come alone." That very afternoon there arrived a hasty note from Aunt Emily announcing that grandfather was ill again, and Mrs. Marron had postponed her return home. Mrs. Flaherty was " as good as gold " in a way, but her knowledge of cookery proved decidedly rudimentary.

"I'll do the cooking myself," resolved Tessie. Alack for her rash self-confidence! Three days had elapsed since Delia's departure; at breakfast on the morning of the fourth Tessie's coffee and buttered toast did not turn out any better than Mrs. Flaherty's attempts, to say nothing of the beefsteak and creamed potatoes.

Mr. Marron tried to observe the agreement not to find fault, but Ben and Joe kept up such a running fire of conundrums anent their sister's culinary efforts that at length papa quietly propounded one in his turn.

"Why are you obstreperous urchins like a railway train about to be side-tracked?" he asked, looking up from his newspaper. Neither could hit upon the correct answer.

"Because you will probably be switched off directly," he explained, with a significant nod, which called forth a laugh from the little girls, and promptly caused the boys to lose all interest in their riddle-making. The meal over, Tessie, after a little prayer for patience, said to herself: "I'll have a nice dessert at dinner to offset my failure this time. I can cook a custard, anyhow." The pudding indeed turned out a complete success. When the gratified young cook threw open the oven door, and revealed the delicacy ready for the table, her two little sisters clapped their hands and Mrs. Flaherty declared it " fine enough to put before a king! "

The boys were favored with a peep at it when they came home from school, and when papa arrived from his counting-room he was at once informed by May and Toosie of the treat to be expected. The shortcomings of the dinner itself were overlooked in anticipation of " the triumph of the confectioner's art," as Joe styled Tessie's masterpiece. But, oh, the pity! How many a mishap may chance between anticipation and fulfilment! As she took the hot dish from the oven it slipped from her hands and fell to the floor. The delectable pudding was irretrievably lost!

" A leprechaun must have been at the making of it to bring such ill-luck!" bewailed Mrs. Flaherty in real distress. Returning to the dining-room, Tessie sank upon a chair, the picture of serio-comic woe; the cherubs wept quietly in mingled sympathy for her trials and their own disappointment.

> " Humpty-dumpty sat on a wall,
> Humpty-dumpty had a great fall;
> Not all the king's horses nor all the king's men
> Could make Humpty-dumpty whole again,"

sang the boys in rueful chorus.

"Never mind, my dear, accidents will happen and you are doing valiantly," attested her father as he lit his after-dinner cigar. Later, however, his young housekeeper shed a few tears "unknown to any one but Judy Flaherty," as the good woman assured her by way of sustaining her courage.

* * * *

"Tessie," remarked Mr. Marron next day, "a friend of mine from New York is in town and I have invited him to tea this evening— just give us a simple supper," he went on, seeing her look of dismay; "I will have a roast turkey sent up from the caterer's."

Tessie's face cleared. "Oh, very well," she said. It was so nice to be able to please papa.

At dusk Mr. Marron returned with his friend, Mr. Taylor, an elderly gentleman whose courtly deference to Tessie as the acting mistress of the house made her feel very important. Before long Mrs. Flaherty in a stiffly starched white apron, dropped an awkward courtesy at the drawing-room door and announced: "Tea is served, miss."

Mr. Taylor, being fond of children, begged that May and Toosie might be placed one on either side of him at table. The boys kicked each other's shins under the mahogany, and Ben confided to his brother in a stage whisper that the stranger was "a jolly old duffer;" at which their elder sister crimsoned, and hoped

the gentleman was afflicted with deafness—
"though wishing him no harm," as Mrs.
Flaherty would have added. Very pretty the
board looked, with its dainty china, snowy
damask, sparkling cut glass, and gleaming
silver. The pleasant air of comfort drew from
Mr. Taylor the remark: "Well, Mr. Marron,
although we miss the presence of your charming
wife, it must be highly gratifying to you
to have her place so admirably filled by your
daughter."

The turkey proved, in Ben's parlance, "a
noble bird." By the time it was replaced by a
dish of delicious-looking sliced oranges and
some of Delia's incomparable fruit-cake Tessie
felt entirely at ease; the children were behaving
beautifully, and she could listen with unconcern
to the conversation, and answer
brightly when the kindly gentleman addressed
her. This playing hostess was certainly agreeable.

"H'm! the oranges need a trifle more
sugar, my dear," suggested her father,
abruptly.

"Yes, father," she replied, passing to the
guest a small Wedgwood bowl shaped like an
Etruscan vase, which she had hastily filled
with powdered sugar a few moments before
they sat down to the meal. The visitor rested
the spoon on the edge of the Etruscan vase a
moment while he spoke to May; then he
sprinkled some of the sugar over the orange

on the little Dresden plate which had been set before him.

But shades of the seven cooks of Paris! what necromancy was here? No sooner had the snowy powder touched the luscious fruit than there was a *puff*—a mysterious fizzing sound—the orange seemed to bubble up, and the plate was enveloped in a sizzling white cloud. Mr. Taylor instinctively drew back.

"Oh, see!" cried Toosie and May together. The boys stared, and quickly broke into a shout of laughter. Mr. Marron frowned in a puzzled way, and turned to Tessie for an explanation; but, blushing with confusion, she could only shake her head, being as unable to account for the phenomenon as were the others. Suddenly a light dawned upon her, however.

"I know now," she stammered, "I must have made a mistake; it is not powdered sugar at all!"

"What then?" demanded her father sternly.

Tessie quailed inwardly; there flashed upon her mind a gruesome mediæval story of a lady who in pretended friendship had bidden her guests to a poisoned banquet. She stole a timid glance at Mr. Taylor, wondering if a like thought had occurred to him. But he was smiling broadly.

"It is just—*baking-powder!*" she gasped, with burning cheeks. "There was a package of baking-powder in the pantry and in my haste I mistook it for the sugar; please excuse my stupidity."

Mr. Marron's annoyance was appeased, and Mr. Taylor threw back his head and "ha, ha'd" good-naturedly.

"I understand," he said; "the bicarbonate of soda in the powder mingling with the acid of the fruit produced an effervescence of course,—ha, ha, ha! But the little pyrotechnic display, although not on the *menu*, does not detract from the many evidences you have given us of your skill as a housekeeper, Miss Tessie."

The boys were still inclined to be hilarious over the practical joke Tessie had played upon herself, the little girls still giggled, but their father by a soft but imperative tap on the table called them to order, as Mrs. Flaherty brought on a fresh supply of oranges profusely sugared.

* * *

A day or two after this misadventure Delia came home, her recovery having perhaps been hastened by her uneasiness lest Mrs. Flaherty might "presume too much" on the footing accorded her in the household. Although still somewhat stiff and lame as the result of the encounter with the bicyclist, she declared herself able to resume her duties, and oh, how happy Tessie was to have her take them up again.

CHAPTER IV.

THE COOKING CLASS.

"I KNEW you would be interested, Tessie, dear, so I came right over to tell you," announced Laura Gaines one morning, as she sank into the most comfortable chair in the Marrons' cosy sitting-room.

"Miss Garnish will be in town for a month to give lessons in cookery; society has taken up the fad, and Mrs. Van Rensaleer is to be the president of a Ladies' Cooking Class, which means, of course, that it will be very select. There is to be a junior class besides. None of the nobodies will be asked to join, only girls who will be débutantes two or three winters from now, like you and me, for instance."

"Oh, I'm not sure that I shall 'come out' formally," disclaimed Tessie, impressed by the picture Laura's imagination thus painted with a few bold strokes.

"No doubt your mother would have heard from Mrs. Van Rensaleer on the subject of the class before this, if she had been at home," pursued her friend with awkward hesitation.

"There is a note from her waiting to be forwarded to mother. I know it from the monogram," answered Tessie quickly, for like many older, and ostensibly wiser, people she was not insensible to the satisfaction of having her family recognized as belonging to the most exclusive social circle of Perryville.

"Yes," agreed Laura, glancing at the envelope which Tessie took from the chimney-piece, and held out for her inspection. "It must be the invitation. But about the junior class—mamma has entered into the plan with great spirit; she says it is such a splendid opportunity for a young girl to learn to cook; what would she not have given for such a chance when she was our age, and so on. As Mrs. Van Rensaleer, having no daughters of her own, is not acquainted with the future society buds, mamma has suggested to her the names of some of the eligible girls. 'There is Tessie Marron to begin with,' she said, and the lady president replied, 'Yes, the Marrons are counted among our very best families.'"

Again Tessie felt a little glow of gratified pride.

"And then," concluded Laura, having paused only to take breath, "as you are really keeping house, you will find the lessons of practical value."

The young housekeeper sighed, recalling her experiences during Delia's absence. "I think it is a very nice plan," she admitted.

"I was sure you would be delighted," ran on Laura; "furthermore it is proposed that once a fortnight each member of the coterie in turn shall invite the others to a luncheon at her house, the dishes served to be prepared by herself. *Sub rosa*, I believe most of the girls will turn the recipes over to their mothers' cooks as the surer way of attaining good results; but at any rate the parties will give us many pleasant Saturday afternoons—for of course we can keep these entertainments up during Lent, you know, since the aim is so domestic and praiseworthy and—and—I really *shall* endeavor to learn to make some new dishes for Fridays and abstinence days, which are *so* trying!"

Evidently pretty, frivolous Laura's realization of the object of the fasts of the Church was even more vague and farther astray than her notion of the advantages to be derived from the lessons in cookery. In fact, like her good-looking, amiable, worldly-minded mother, she wished to glide through life as easily as possible, and make everything she undertook a social success.

"Really, I must be going," she now exclaimed, starting up; "I came in for a few minutes and have stayed an hour; but you are always *so* entertaining. You will arrange about the class, won't you? Ten dollars for the course; so cheap, is it not?"

Thus chatter, chatter, ran on Laura's treble

but not unmusical voice, as she fluttered into the handsome coat she had thrown off upon her arrival, drew on her gloves with various little jerks, and, lightly touching Tessie's cheek in a bird-like manner, supposed to be indicative of intense affection, took her departure, leaving her dearest friend slightly bewildered, but in a whirl of pleasurable excitement. "It is a nice plan," repeated Tessie to herself, her thoughts occupied more especially with the social features of the scheme, whereon Laura had dwelt so enthusiastically, for the girls of their set dearly loved to provide amusement for the precious Saturday afternoons after the work of the week at school.

"And then, too, I am truly anxious to learn how to cook," she continued. "It will be so useful, and economical, too, in the end, if I can prepare the delicious confections for which Miss Garnish is noted. Mother will not need to engage the services of a caterer for my début in two years' time, for of course, as Laura says, I shall be *obliged* to have a coming out party. I shall speak to father about the lessons after tea."

In the evening, accordingly, when the boys had vanished to the upper regions, the cherubs were asleep in their little beds, and Mr. Marron, established at ease before the sitting-room fire, was tranquilly puffing at his cigar, she preferred her request.

The Cooking Class. 43

"What, pay ten dollars to learn to make flimflams and flummery!" he muttered, impatiently; for it was an inopportune time, early in January, when business men are apt to have obligations to meet, and this year for many people "money was tight," as the saying is.

"But, father," alleged Tessie, somewhat offended that he took so small account of her good intentions, "it would be so useful—"

"Fudge!" he commented, unappreciatively: "your mother never attended a cooking school."

"No, but she will have an opportunity now," responded his daughter naïvely.

Mr. Marron threw himself back in his chair, and began to laugh immoderately. With an air of offended dignity Tessie seated herself on an ottoman at the other side of the reading-table, and picking up a magazine fixed her eyes upon an illustration without the faintest idea of what she was looking at. Presently her father, controlling his amusement, leaned forward, and, regarding her seriously, said:

"My dear child, these classes are all very well in their way, but if you are in earnest about learning to cook you could not have a better school than the home kitchen, nor a more competent instructor than Delia. As for your mother, in my opinion she is better versed in the science than most of those who lecture upon it. I dare say Mrs. Gaines, however, might profit by the lessons, to judge from Gaines' fondness for dining at the Gentlemen's Club."

Tessie inwardly resented the criticism upon Laura's mother.

"To learn at home would not be the same," she replied, biting the corner of her dainty handkerchief. "You do not understand—"

Mr. Marron dismissed the subject, however, and became engrossed in a newspaper, leaving her to lapse into moody silence.

"Why had she not settled the question with her mother?" she asked herself in chagrin, for she rightly surmised that Mrs. Marron, being unwilling to deprive her of any advantage or diversion enjoyed by her companions, would have arranged that the ten dollars should be forthcoming. The next day, feeling the need of sympathy, she told her disappointment to Delia.

"Faith, and a right view your father took," declared her humble confidant, with a wise nod of the head. "These coolinary seeances, or whatever they are called, may do for those whose early education—what with painting, music, and the like—has been *neglected*. But if you want to ask your friends to a luncheon, I'll teach you how to prepare a royal one. To tell you the truth, Miss Tessie, I've had hopes that, with the experience you are getting willy-nilly, as one may say, and the worries you had by reason of your ignorance while I was away, you *would* start in and take a genuine interest in housekeeping. There's your mother, now; if I am extra busy she will come down and make a loaf of cake—perhaps for the friends you have in to tea—and think nothing of it. 'Sure, it's Miss Tessie who ought to learn to do that,' I sometimes say to her, but she always answers: 'Do not mention it, Delia; the child has enough to see to, with her studies and her music.'

"'There's the vacations and Saturdays when she lolls in the sitting-room with a story book and complains of having nothing to do,' I argify. Like as not at this the mistress draws herself up with a grand air and says: 'We won't discuss the point further, if you please,' and I feel put in my place without more ado."

Tessie wished for a share of Mrs. Marron's quiet dignity to check her plain-spoken counsellor now; but her conscience was uneasy and she made no reply.

"'Yes indeed,' I says to myself," the much-humored servant went on, "'what is the good of book knowledge and all the arts and sceances if a girl does not learn to spare her mother? And how is it that Miss Tessie—who is so pious in her way—comes in and out day after day, when her mother is at home, with no thought but of her own concerns?'"

Tessie burst into tears; it seemed to her that her good resolutions of the last few weeks had been productive of very little fruit after all.

"How selfish I have been, Delia," she acknowledged contritely. "Dear mother, what an unloving, negligent child she has!"

At sight of the young girl's compunction Delia melted at once.

"Not at all," she averred, veering round completely; "who can show a prettier or a better daughter than is Tessie Marron? Whisht, alanna! or it is the 'sterics [hysterics] you will be having directly! Bad cess to my rambling tongue that is too ready by half; ah, but it is the good heart you have, asthore! Whisht, don't cry; give me the good heart, says I, and the seed sown there will yield a generous harvest. I ask your pardon, miss, for speaking so; sure, would not the mistress be put out with me if she knew. She was right, as she always is; too heavy a burden must not be put on young shoulders, or young folk be blamed too much if they are a bit thoughtless, sometimes. Indeed, it is wonderfully well you have done since your mother has been away, and great credit is due to you for it."

"Truly, I *have* tried," faltered Tessie, drying her eyes, and very willing to be comforted; "but often, as you say, Delia, I just don't think. No doubt I appeared very pettish and unreasonable to father last night. I must not let myself be so taken up with every fad the girls start, but be more considerate for dear

mother, who forgets herself for all of us. I
will take the cooking lessons from you and
surprise her when she comes home. I know
she will readily let me give the little luncheon
—for she always says simple, unpretending
hospitality, according to one's means, is a
Christian virtue to be practised as well as a
pleasure to be availed of; and my friends will
be glad to come even if I do not belong to
their cooking class."

CHAPTER V.

TWO YOUNG HOSTESSES.

Mrs. Marron's visit to New York was prolonged by the continued illness of her father, for, as the latter was loath to have her leave him, Mr. Marron counselled her to remain, reporting that all was going well at home. Meantime, Tessie profited by her resolution to cultivate a taste for domestic accomplishments; the house now wore a neater air, and under Delia's supervision she had learned to prepare various dainty dishes. Several of her friends also preferred to take lessons in cookery as she was doing, but Miss Garnish's circle flourished, Laura Gaines being one of that lady's most enthusiastic pupils. When Laura's turn came for entertaining the class, she decided in favor of a "high tea" instead of a luncheon.

"It will evidently be an elaborate affair," Tessie wrote to her mother, and Mrs. Marron, with ready understanding of a girl's longings on such occasions said in reply: "I am sorry I am not at hand, dear, to help you in any little preparations you may need to make for Laura's party. If you like you may take your crimson frock to our usual dressmaker, Miss Beaubien, and tell her to procure a few yards of silk and retrim it; I will attend to the bill upon my return."

Delighted at this permission, Tessie studied a fashion magazine for the greater part of a morning. She had finally chosen the style according to which the frock should be remodelled, when suddenly came the recollection of the day when her mother was getting ready to go away—her dissatisfaction with the plain bonnet, and her determination that "all the pretty things" should no longer be bought for herself and the little girls. Taking from her wardrobe the crimson frock, she contemplated it with a critical eye.

"After all, it is very pretty as it is," she conceded at length, yet not without one more wistful glance at the fashion-plate. "'Twas new in the autumn and I have only worn it a few times; I believe I will not mind about enlisting the services of Miss Beaubien, or get the extra silk; with some ribbons and a fresh bit of lace, it will do very well."

The little sacrifice cost her a sigh, but when she was dressed for the party a last glance at the mirror was pleasing enough to satisfy her, for the warm, deep color of the simple frock set off admirably her pale complexion, dark eyes, and soft brown hair.

Mrs. Gaines and Laura received in elaborate evening gowns, however, and several of the young guests were more richly attired than was suitable for schoolgirls. As she mingled with them Tessie felt a momentary regret at not having adopted mamma's suggestion, but she generously put away the thought, and Emily Carrington's impulsive whisper: "My dear, you look like a picture,"—a compliment which coming somewhat in the nature of a reward—quickly restored her equanimity.

Laura's tea was indeed a gorgeous entertainment. The table was laid with an imported cloth that cost two hundred dollars, the appointments were correspondingly sumptuous, and the viands, perhaps fortunately, were not prepared by the delicate, beringed hands of the youthful hostess, but, as she frankly acknowledged, ordered from the Delmonico's of Perryville.

"Very splendid," observed the irrepressible Emily, aside to Tessie, "but this formality and atmosphere of society appear to weigh upon the spirits of the company; none of the girls are a bit natural, and for my part I should like to scream aloud, or go about sticking pins in them to frighten them out of their stiffness."

Tessie glanced at her apprehensively, as with a smile she rattled on.

"Mrs. Gaines is awfully good-natured, but is it not execrable taste to make such a splurge over a schoolgirl party? Rather unrefined, don't you think so?"

Tessie winced; pleased as she was with the richness and glitter that met her eyes upon all sides, a similar reflection had passed through her own mind. But she was her mother's daughter, and Mrs. Marron was considered by many as the most perfectly well-bred woman in Perryville.

"Don't you think so?" reiterated Emily, with a nudge.

"Having accepted a friend's hospitality, I think it would be the worst possible taste for me to criticise her entertainment," she replied coldly.

Emily colored and stammered, with an uneasy laugh.

"Oh! I forgot I was talking to Laura's dearest companion. Still, I am sure you won't repeat what I said. It is not kind or ladylike to comment upon whatever arrangements one's hostess chooses to make, I admit, although so many people do it, and I only gave you the benefit of a remark made to me several times since I came into the room. Anyhow this will probably spoil the whole plan of the pleasant afternoons; the other girls will not care to entertain the class if they cannot make as grand a display, and very few can, you know."

Emily flitted away to join Irene Wier; but Tessie, half hidden behind an oriental portière, remained lost in thought. She had intended to invite her friends to luncheon that day fortnight, but in truth the extravagant lavishness of the present scene had produced upon her just the impression Emily had described.

The next day, being still undecided, she determined, since her mother was absent, to consult the latter's dear friend, Miss Langdon, who had been a belle and a beauty in her day and still, at intervals, gave delightful at homes in the charming old Langdon mansion, where she also presided over the most fashionable school in Perryville.

"By all means give your little party," advised this lady cordially, "If Laura's tea was too ostentatious, we will ascribe the mistake to the generosity and good-heartedness of her mother and herself. But by bringing your friends together in a spirit of unpretending hospitality, your independence will encourage them to do likewise and keep up the pleasant round of Saturday reunions."

So Tessie sent out invitations, and wrote to her mother of her decision. Mrs. Marron's return letter contained an enclosure, of which she said: "Grandfather is much interested in your party and insists upon sending a check to provide a few 'extras' in the way of flowers and bonbons."

The check was a liberal one and the young girl was delighted.

"I shall have everything very nice without any attempt at show," she said to herself, "and although two or three of the girls may perhaps make unfavorable comparisons between my party and Laura's, I'll try not to mind, but do my best to make every one have a good time."

The momentous day came at last, and Tessie, in a flutter of excitement, awaited her guests in the drawing-room of the little Dutch house, which, with all its antiquated homeliness, she dearly loved. Miss Langdon had kindly offered to superintend behind the scenes; a cousin of Delia's, a competent waitress temporarily out of place, had been pressed into service; and all preparations for the entertainment were completed. This agreeable consciousness caused the young hostess to recover quickly from her nervousness when her guests actually began to arrive, and she welcomed them with something of her mother's easy courtesy.

Pretty enough for a fairy banquet was the luncheon table, with its handsome appointments set off by the roses at each place—provided out of grandfather's check—the little menu cards painted by Tessie herself, and the many candles with their rose-colored silken caps or shades.

The waitress fully equalled her reputation, Delia's cookery even surpassed its usual excellence, and Tessie knew that the "angel cake" she had made herself was a complete success. The arrangements manifestly met with general approval, and yet, despite all this, as at Laura's, though certainly not for the reason Emily had given, a chill formality settled down upon the company like a filmy cloud. They seemed to feel that Laura's tea had launched them into society and they must behave like other beings than their natural selves. Hence the friends who were accustomed to meet familiarly every day were as prim as though some malignant pixie, offended at not being asked to the party, had cast a spell upon them. Even Emily, usually so voluble, had nothing to say, and Laura's thoughts appeared to be engrossed by the gown she wore, a gown from New York, quite ahead of the prevailing fashion in Perryville.

The dulness was becoming oppressive, and the hostess was well-nigh in despair, when suddenly there was an ominous scuffle on the veranda and Joe's voice was heard calling: "Hold on, she is not quite ready."

"Oh, there is no use in putting too big a shine on her," was the reply from Ben.

The next moment, Tessie's eyes being attracted to the window opposite, she beheld a spectacle which nearly caused her to drop the cup of chocolate she was just raising to her lips in an attempt to appear at ease. There, framed by the old-fashioned casement, like a caricature from a comic magazine, stood Joe, holding aloft a struggling, squirming creature of about the size and shape of a large ape.

What could it be ? There was not a monkey in the town—

Alas, after the first shock of amazement she recognized through the hideous disguise *her beautiful pet cat Ermine !*

But what a transformation ! Ermine, whose snowy whiteness had been ever the pride of her mistress, and who, with the daintiness of her namesake, shrank from contact with aught that would leave the slightest speck upon her soft fur—Ermine was now as black as any Nubian. How had the rogues metamorphosed her ?

At another time their sister would have made a dash at them, and speedily called them to account. How trying it was to be obliged to remain apparently oblivious, hoping the capers of the young scapegrace without would escape notice, and that having played his prank he would disappear to chuckle over it with Ben. But Joe had no intention of going away; moreover Ben himself presently appeared to complete the tableau, and then, as if this were not enough, began a fandango, Joe promptly joining in the dance and swinging poor Ermine to and fro to imaginary music.

The exhibition was intended solely for Tessie's benefit, but she was not destined to be its only spectator.

"Why, what was that ?" cried Laura, looking up with a start and finding her voice at last, as the shadow of the performers obscured the sunlight which had been streaming into the room.

As the comical picture met her gaze she began to laugh uncontrollably. The other girls glanced quickly first at Tessie's flushed face and compressed lips, then towards the window at which Laura was staring. Before they could recover from their astonishment sufficiently to join in the latter's merriment, there followed a *dénouement* not on the program of the teasing perpetrators of this practical joke. Distracted by the antics of the boys and the mauling she had received, poor Ermine, catching sight of her kind mistress, by a desperate lurch broke free from her tormentors, and leaped with all her strength against the window. The pane cracked—gave way, and shivering the glass into a hundred pieces the frightened animal plunged into the room.

At the same moment Ben called out in real concern: "O Tessie, we did not intend this! We blackened Ermine with your French shoe-polish and she looked so funny we thought we would show her to you on the quiet. We did not suppose she would want to go to your luncheon without an invitation!"

Thereupon the two mischief-makers scampered away.

Poor Tessie! Her friends, who had started up in alarm, were on the point of beating a retreat, but Margaret, Delia's cousin, with ready energy came to the rescue. Picking up the cowering, trembling cat, she cried:

"Sure, miss, the creature is not hurt; only a bit scratched and bewildered. As for their making a naiger of her—well, well, I've seen more than one turncoat in my day, but if this does not beat them all!"

Her loud aside caused a general diversion, and as she disappeared kitchenward, carrying away the luckless intruder, the girls, having recovered from their consternation, broke into a peal of mirth. Tessie was unable to appreciate the ludicrous side of the affair, however, and could hardly keep back the tears of vexation that sprang to her eyes.

"Ben and Joe are the *meanest* of brothers!" she said to herself, resentfully. Had she been at liberty to pursue, and chanced to capture them, no doubt she would have expressed her opinion of their conduct in terms more forcible than gentle. But the experience proved to the much-tried girl that the necessity of self-control, imposed by social requirements, is very useful as far as it goes. Without doubt, too, her frequent efforts of late to be patient and forbearing helped her in this extremity of her mortification. With an effort to join in the laugh, she resumed her place at the table; the guests followed her example, and now, to her pleased surprise, the whole atmosphere seemed changed, every one became bright and gay. What droll anecdotes

Ermine's ridiculous plight called forth! Before long the young hostess was really laughing unaffectedly, with a comfortable sense that her party was a success after all.

Presently the little company repaired to the drawing-room, and, having by this time thoroughly succeeded in thrusting her annoyance into the background, Tessie sat down at the piano and rattled off inspiriting music, while her friends joined in a lively dance, chasséeing out into the hall and to the sitting-room beyond. They had games, too, and no end of amusement, until Laura, peeping at her toy-like chatelaine watch, exclaimed: "Girls, it is actually five o'clock!" Then the party broke up.

"It is so jolly, I just hate to go, though," said Emily Carrington, bluntly.

"I never had a better time in my life," declared Laura, kissing Tessie on both cheeks in bidding her "Good-by until to-morrow."

"And you would take a prize in cookery over all Miss Garnish's pupils," averred Irene Wier.

* * * *

When they had all gone, and Tessie sought out Delia to thank her for taking so much trouble to have everything right, she found the good woman still highly indignant at the boys for their escapade.

"'Tis seldom I complain of them, but their father shall hear of the disgrace they were to you this day, my dear," she said; " Miss Langdon was astonished at their behavior, so she told them, before she went home."

Nevertheless, Tessie, with the congratulations of her friends still ringing in her ears, was now disposed to judge the culprits more leniently than at first, and begged her irate champion to let the matter pass. Yet the broken window was awkwardly conspicuous, and the " deep-dyed villain of a cat," as Joe called her, would not be kept out of the way. These damaging evidences against the boys did not fail to attract the attention of Mr. Marron, and he put such leading questions to his sons that they were forced to " own up."

But their sister interceded to save them from punishment.

"Pray overlook the prank, father," she pleaded generously; " after all it won the day for me. Only something very unexpected could have broken down the barrier of stiffness, as impassable as the great wall of China, which seemed to separate each girl from her neighbor."

Tessie had her way; but although she forgave her brothers, for some days a queer, foolish lump came in her throat every time she looked at Ermine, whose furry coat took on as many shades as Joseph's historic garment, especially the faded greenery-yellowy, indigo-mauve tints beloved by pre-Raphaelites, before it again resumed its own snowy whiteness.

CHAPTER VI.

MISS LANGDON'S SCHOOL.

THERE was no convent academy in Perryville, but during the autumn previous to the events just narrated the aristocratic and once wealthy Miss Langdon had opened a select school in the stately residence that had been the home of her childhood. There were a few boarding pupils, but the majority were day scholars; she herself exercised a general supervision and presided over the most advanced class; the other classes were taught by subordinates, and special professors gave instruction in music, painting, and elocution.

As before arranged by Mrs. Marron, Tessie and also little May began to attend this school after the Christmas holidays. Several of their friends had been coming here since October, and these now welcomed them with enthusiasm.

"I believe you are to enter our class," said Laura Gaines to Tessie, as the girls hung up their jackets and hats at the end of the corridor.

"Yes, it was decided yesterday," was the happy answer.

"Well, I am delighted that we are to be together; but for your sake, my dear, I am sorry Miss Langdon is not our teacher, because Miss Carstens—" and Laura elevated her eyebrows, as though at a loss for words to describe the latter personage.

The time-mellowed voice of an antique clock striking the hour of nine caused the loiterers to repair in haste to the study hall, once the drawing-room of the old house.

The stiff-backed, brocatel-covered furniture of other days had been removed, but the crystal chandeliers, that had flashed their radiance upon many a gay company, now caught the morning sunbeams, and rained them upon the floor of polished oak in a shower of prismatic colors; the mantel mirrors and the long pier-glasses repeated again and again the fresh young faces before them, as if pleased to transmit such bright reflections; and upon the walls hung several valuable paintings. Of these latter the most attractive was a large picture at the end of the room, representing the "Girlhood of Mary."

Miss Langdon had been educated at a convent in France, and the secret of the charm she exerted over all who approached her lay doubtless in the counsel often repeated to her charges. "Learn to imitate the courtesy as well as the gentleness of Our Blessed Lady," she was wont to say to them; "try to be considerate, self-forgetful, and kind as She was;

model your manners after hers, in short, and you will attain the sweet dignity appropriate even to young girls, and the perfection of womanly grace."

Tessie was given a place next to Laura. When the classes were called she followed her deskmate to the recitation-room, slightly nervous over the prospect before her, for Laura's description of what she might expect had certainly not been encouraging. Miss Carstens proved to be a small, austere personage, with a sharp, colorless face, cold blue eyes framed by steel-rimmed spectacles, and firm, thin lips. Her opening remark after the short prayer with which the exercises began was not calculated to dispel the chilling impression caused by her severe aspect.

"So we are together again," she said, as the class ranged their chairs around her green baize-covered table, "and we may consider ourselves fortunate in having no new pupil among us, since thus no time need be lost in explaining the rules."

Emily fidgeted; Laura coughed warningly.

"Order, if you please!" The little teacher looked up at them sharply, and became aware of the presence of a stranger. Leisurely settling her spectacles, she regarded the newcomer with a stony stare, and observed coldly: "My dear, is there not some misunderstanding? I had no intimation that you were to be under my instruction."

For reply Tessie passed to her a card whereon Miss Langdon had written " Second English Class."

Miss Carstens compressed her lips; it was not pleasant to find that the mistake was hers.

" Be seated, my dear," she snapped, still more frigidly. " I doubt if you will be able to keep up with us, however; to enter in the middle of a term is always a disadvantage."

Disconcerted, Tessie shrank back into her place.

" Just like the old iceberg," muttered Laura, giving her hand a reassuring squeeze; " but she is not always so formidable—sometimes she unbends a little if all goes well."

The lessons had scarce begun when they were interrupted by the appearance of Miss Langdon herself, accompanied by a diffident, round-shouldered girl, who was so plainly dressed as to be almost shabby.

" Miss Carstens," breezily began Madame (for so she was formally addressed), " I must apologize for having neglected to inform you that I had assigned a new pupil to this class. Now I have brought you another. This is Mary Renwick; I am sure you will make her feel at home."

" Oh, yes, to be sure," commented Laura sarcastically, under her breath, as she sketched the awe-inspiring spectacles upon the margin of her algebra.

Perhaps Miss Carstens understood the request to be in reality a counsel; perhaps the appealing glance of Mary's dark eyes penetrated even her reserve—for the "my dear" that welcomed this awkward young person was several degrees warmer than that which had snubbed Tessie a few moments before. From the beginning the eccentric woman seemed perversely intent upon contrasting one new pupil with the other. Mary, when called upon to recite, forgot her shyness so far as to acquit herself creditably, but Tessie, not having recovered self-possession, failed almost every time a question was put to her.

"It is as I said. Had you not better go down to the third class, my dear?" suggested Miss Carstens at the close of the hour.

"Oh, I failed because everything is so strange to me yet," was the quick response.

"But Mary Renwick did not fail, and everything is strange to her also."

"I will try to do better to-morrow," Tessie promised in desperation.

Nevertheless, the poor child had so many small worries at home, owing to her mother's unavoidably long absence, her time for study was so broken in upon, and the consciousness that she had not begun well with Miss Carstens was so disheartening, that her recitations continued faulty day after day and every excuse she offered was met by the same cool rejoinder from her teacher: "But Mary Renwick does not do so, and *she* is a new pupil, too."

"I am growing to detest Mary Renwick," she avowed to Laura, as they promenaded during recreation in the garden.

"How that individual managed to get into the good graces of the snow image I cannot imagine," responded her friend sympathetically.

"I wonder she was accepted here as a pupil anyhow," chimed in Emily Carrington, who joined them just in time to catch the name of the personality under discussion; "her father is only a clerk in the office of Lane & Co.'s furniture-store, and the family live in a small house on Vine Street and are quite poor, I have been told. I dare say Miss Langdon has taken Mary without charge."

"Humph! Madame need not attempt to palm off her protégée upon us, then," asserted Laura, with a shrug of the shoulders; "mamma is very particular that I should associate only with the *best* people."

"Well, I cannot *endure* the girl," proclaimed Tessie with still more emphasis, "and I never shall!"

As time went on, however, she began to be a little troubled in regard to her aversion towards the quiet, retiring stranger, who after all had not willingly wronged her in the slightest instance.

For who could long withstand the silent influence of the study-room, where at the end of the rows of desks appeared the sweet form of the Immaculate Maid of the Temple, with her book and her spinning, come, as it were, to be the companion of the young girls assembled here, in their studies and their work.

One day as Tessie's eyes glanced from the picture to where the pensive face of her rival bent over the history lesson, there dawned upon her a sudden realization of the difference between the haughtiness of her own manner and the winning gentleness of the "most gracious among women."

"I do not like that Renwick girl!" she said *sotto voce*, "but"—the remainder of the sentence was confided to the page before her and lost amid the confusion of a pitched battle between the Greeks and the Romans.

"I have hit upon a plan to get the better of my dislike of Mary Renwick," she confided to Laura, on the way home from school.

"And what is that, pray?" inquired the latter, with some curiosity.

"Of course it is not Mary's fault that Miss Carstens is always holding her up as a model to me, and so, instead of visiting my vexation upon her, I am going to avail myself of every little chance to be agreeable and obliging towards her."

Laura stared incredulously, and then broke out with:

"Well, you *are* the queerest character I ever knew, Tessie Marron! What next?"

"Yes," proceeded Tessie earnestly, absorbed in her project, "one cannot dislike anybody all the time when one is trying to be nice to her; and then I am partly to blame for the way Mary has been slighted in the school. My friends have, naturally, taken sides with me, you see—"

"Oh, to be sure you may do as you please, *mon amie*," interrupted Laura curtly; "but because you now intend to cultivate the acquaintance of this little upstart you must not expect *our set* to do so. *Au revoir!* I congratulate you upon your new friend."

The next afternoon Mary Renwick, as she sat at her desk after school endeavoring to finish a composition, found her thoughts dwelling in bitter disappointment upon the ill-will towards herself which she had unwittingly aroused among her schoolmates.

"And I hoped it would be so different!" she sadly soliloquized.

Mary was her father's housekeeper. In the past she had learned her lessons at home and repeated them to her mother, but Mrs. Renwick was often ill and all books were put aside. Then the dear mother died and for a time afterwards everything was a blank.

The first ray of life's sunshine for Mary again came when it was decided that she and her little brother should go to school. How pleasant it was the first morning when, having left Willie at the kindergarten, she went on to Miss Langdon's. In what a flutter of excitement and pleasure she was at the prospect of having companions of her own age. During the study hour how the words of the lesson seemed to dance all over the leaves of the book, and at odd moments with what interest her gaze strayed from her task!

"These girls, who look so happy and attractive, and wear such pretty gowns, will surely be sweet and friendly," she said to herself. Then came class, and she was so grateful for Miss Carstens' encouragement. But, alas, recreation-time brought disillusion. Two or three of the most sociable of the pupils asked her how she liked the school, but the others took no notice of her, and before long she was left sitting alone on a bench under one of the trees of the garden. And thus it had been ever since. She was hardly better acquainted with her schoolmates now than at first.

"I wish I knew how to make friends, because I like some of the girls so much," she sighed: "but, heighho! I must not mope over it. Of what account are my small trials at school after all, so long as everything goes well at home? Father and Willie do not think me odd or strange, as these girls seem to, and father praises me when I try to plan and sew my gowns; he does not laugh when I do not get them exactly right or according to the latest fashion. How delighted he is, too, when I win high rank in class! Since it is to please him I am working, why should I fret over the little spiteful ways of some of the girls? I am not going to do so; I would not for anything have father know I am not perfectly happy here. He tells me so often how gratified he is that I have the advantage of associating with those who are perfect ladies in every respect. H'm, how indignant he would be if he knew of the manner in which they act towards me! Is it because father is poor, and I cannot wear pretty gowns? Or because dear Miss Carstens has unconsciously made Tessie Marron heartily dislike me? I know Tessie thinks me a prig, and mean, and disagreeable. Yet how can I help it? Fudge! I do not intend to bother about the matter any more. I must go now and look up those points in connection with to-morrow's history lesson upon which we are expected to be informed."

CHAPTER VII.

MARY RENWICK.

PUTTING away her work, Mary repaired to the library, a pleasant room lined from floor to ceiling with the several thousand volumes (many of them rare early editions) collected by Miss Langdon's father. To these the older pupils were allowed access.

As the studious girl softly pushed open the door of this quite retreat, she saw that some one was seated at the long table, bending over a bulky folio.

It was Tessie Marron.

A shadow passed over Mary's face, and at the same moment her rival looked up with a frown.

"What a bore," mentally ejaculated Tessie. "To be confronted with my *bête noir*, as Laura would say, and no good chance to escape, either, for I must finish taking these notes. I need not speak to her, anyhow! Of course we are here on the same errand. Well," she bent her head over the book to hide a smile: "my lady will have some difficulty in finding the information she wants."

For some minutes the newcomer vainly hunted through encyclopedias; then in indecision stood contemplating the rows of shelves.

"Ha, mademoiselle," thought Tessie, "without a doubt you will fail to-morrow. I fancy I hear Miss Carstens saying: 'What, Mary, you could not inform yourself upon this matter? Why, Tessie Marron did so!' But pshaw! Miss Carstens would never say it; she is too partial to her favorite."

Just then the small voice of her inner consciousness whispered: "Tessie, Tessie! what was it you made up your mind to do? Here is a chance to be generous—to put into effect your good resolution."

The two girls had not exchanged a word, but Mary once or twice glanced inquiringly at the book over which her companion pored in affected unconcern. At last Tessie rose, and pushing the volume towards her, said indifferently:

"If you are searching for a description of the manners and customs of the ancient Romans perhaps you may find it here."

A quick smile of pleasure lighted up the thoughtful countenance of the other girl.

"Oh, thank you," she replied, eagerly scanning the page.

This cordial acknowledgment of a trifling courtesy smote her classmate with compunction, however, for the latter felt she had passed the book only lest Mary might suppose she wanted to keep the information to herself.

"It—it is very brief and unsatisfactory, though," continued Mary, after a pause.

Again Tessie hesitated; again interposed that troublesome, persistent little inner counsellor: "Be generous. Do not throw away this opportunity; of course you have a perfect right to do so—you are not obliged to help your rival. It is none of your affair that she may be discomfited to-morrow, but—there are some things better than class points. The vanquishing of a competitor is sweet, but a triumph over one's self is sweeter."

A moment more and the struggle was over; with a light laugh she sprang up, saying: "Yes, it is unsatisfactory, but you will find a much fuller account in a volume on the third shelf, that small book in the brown binding—there, you have it now."

Mary turned around with the book in her hand. "You were kind to tell me," she said gratefully.

"I discovered it by the merest chance myself," explained Tessie.

"I should never have expected—" Mary began awkwardly. Tessie interrupted with some bruskness: "I know; you supposed me mean enough to keep the advantage to myself."

"That is not it," stammered Mary, flushing; but after a second of embarrassment she went on steadily: "We seem fated to misunderstand each other, Tessie, but I have often wanted to tell you how sorry I am that Miss Carstens—"

"I do not care to discuss Miss Carstens," was the cold rejoinder.

"I only meant—"

"It is of no consequence," persisted Tessie, nonchalantly turning over the leaves of an atlas; then, realizing that she was still ungracious, she added, by way of changing the subject of conversation and thus paving the way for an amicable retreat:

"I presume you study very hard?"

"Yes, I do," admitted Mary frankly; "I have to make up for lost time; until I came here I had never attended a regular school."

"Is that what makes you so different from other girls?"

"Am I so different?"

"Why, yes; at least I have always thought so."

"Perhaps it is because I never had any companions of my own age before," said Mary, with an unconscious sigh. "I never missed them while mother lived, because we were company for each other. But I do not know very well what other girls are interested in, or like to talk about, and I cannot get over feeling strange among them."

Tessie's heart was filled with self-reproach,

as she felt how little she and her friends had done to soften this sense of isolation and loneliness for the motherless girl, whose shy reserve was now so quickly melting away beneath the sunshine of a little act of friendliness. They continued chatting until the bell rang for study ten minutes later, and separated, each more kindly disposed towards the other than either would have thought possible half an hour before.

* * * *

"It works like a charm," Tessie acknowledged to Laura a week later. "Since I have tried to be obliging in little ways to Mary Renwick my bitterness against her seems to have died out. Of course when Miss Carstens quotes her virtues for my benefit I am vexed, but after a moment I can laugh over it as one of the iceberg's peculiarities."

"Perhaps your tolerance is due to the fact that you get on so much better in class now," suggested her companion archly.

"Perhaps so; still, I really begin to think Mary is rather a nice girl after all."

"Oh, you are welcome to your opinion, but the other girls have no notion of taking her up because you choose to unbend towards her, my dear," retorted Laura, in a tone which rendered farther discussion of the question inadvisable; fo. Tessie had by no means reached the point of being willing to risk an estrangement from her dearest friend for Mary's sake.

But although her liking for the latter grew stronger every day, the majority of her classmates made the quiet new scholar feel only too keenly that she did not belong to their set. One day when Laura, Emily Carrington, and Irene Wier were chatting together at recreation, Mary, reflecting that perhaps she was too inclined to imagine slights, ventured to join them. In the course of a minute or two the conversation drifted to the subject of dress, as usual when led by butterfly Laura.

With surprising powers of description the three girls discoursed upon their fashionable costumes, past, present, and prospective, covertly eying their companion's simple attire the while.

"And how are you going to have your new frock made, Mary?" inquired Emily, turning to her at last.

"Time enough to decide when I get it," was the careless answer. Mary had a fair share of independence, and was a cheery little creature in the main.

"What! not a modish one, even for the spring?" asked Irene.

"Why do you not have pretty clothes like the rest of us? Why do you wear such queer, old-fashioned gowns?" interjected Laura.

From the clear eyes turned towards her there flashed a scornful glance which caused her to change color, and try to laugh off the rude speech.

"I do not ask my father to buy new dresses for me, because he has too many other expenses," Mary returned bravely.

"Oh, but mamma says 'to be well gowned is a duty we owe to ourselves and to society,'" glibly contended her inquisitor.

"Well gowned, yes, but not more handsomely than one is able to afford," insisted Mary; "I could not pay the bills of a stylish dressmaker, and—and I do try to be neat, but —well, no doubt I *would* make a better appearance if I had a mother to plan and sew for me."

The pathos and rebuke in the words embarrassed her hearers; they were also uncomfortably conscious that they were only too apt to tease for everything they wanted at home. Laura, in some confusion, despite her assumption of what she was pleased to term *sang froid*, murmured a hasty "I beg your pardon" and began to chatter about something else.

* * * *

"What horribly bad taste of Mary to speak so bluntly," remarked Irene to Emily afterwards; "but it served Laura right—although the random shot must have struck home there with particular force. Only this morning I heard father say to mother that the business affairs of Mr. Gaines are not in as good a condition as they might be, and his family are too extravagant by far."

"I heard something of the kind also," affirmed Emily; "Laura would better take care; 'pride goes before a fall' and 'people who live in glass houses,' you know—"

"It made me sorry when Mary spoke of having no mother," continued Irene.

"Yes, but I wonder who does make her frocks!" speculated the irrepressible Emily.

The trio had not meant to be really unkind; because Mary suffered their neglect with gentle dignity they never imagined how deeply it wounded her. And yet, notwithstanding their selfish thoughtlessness, with strange inconsistency, none were so fond as these same girls of bringing little gifts for the adornment of the shrine before the picture in the study room. Irene, for instance, presented the delicately tinted candles she had received at Christmas; Emily, a pair of exquisite porcelain vases; and Laura always provided flowers.

"We have plenty in the conservatory," she was wont to say; "and mamma does not care how many I take, so long as I leave a few blooms to decorate the dinner-table."

By degrees, however, the friends were to be reminded of the "rarer offerings, costing something—but not gold."

* * * *

"I have to stay in after school to rehearse my part in the French charades with Miss Langdon," said Laura, as she nodded good-by to Tessie and Emily one day soon after the spirited passage of arms recorded above. When she returned to the study-room there at a desk sat Mary Renwick, poring over some unfinished task. With a supercilious inclination of the head she passed on, and sitting down at some little distance began to con over the lines of the play.

But her mind often wandered, for she was not happy. Unfortunately the report about the business troubles of Mr. Gaines had some foundation; they were, he hoped, only temporary, but he had informed his wife and daughter very decidedly that their expenditures must be retrenched; there must be no more entertaining on a lavish scale, no more dressmakers' bills for a while.

"Just to think of it!" Laura had bemoaned to herself at this announcement, for she could not even have the satisfaction of talking the matter over with Tessie; "just to think of it! I have had nothing new this winter except that little evening frock for the tea, and the one I was wearing, which I got for Tessie's luncheon. Soon I shall have to fall back upon my old gowns of last year. Well, papa shall see how *horrid* I look; he will be *shamed* into getting me something more *à la mode.*"

Papa was too preoccupied to be impressed as anticipated, but following up this foolish resolution Laura had for a week or more worn one of the last season's frocks with a martyrlike submission in the family circle, and at school in a disdainful defiance of criticism. But for the vague rumors afloat and the fact that she was usually arrayed in the very height of fashion her schoolmates would hardly have remarked the difference, and as it was they attached much less importance to the circumstance than she imagined. But Laura was sensitive and now her thoughts ran on as follows:

"Oh, dear, I need not have sneered at Mary on account of her shabby clothes," she sighed; "soon I may be as dowdy as she is, and my friends will slight me as I have slighted her. How she keeps scrutinizing me! Of course she is meditating how she can retaliate for all the mean things I have said and done to her. Oh, dear, oh, dear, perhaps we shall become *really poor*, and have to live in a second-rate neighborhood, and never have anything nice again, and I shall always look just as horrid as I do to-day."

The eyes of the despondent girl filled with tears. At this moment, glancing up, she encountered Mary's gaze still steadily fixed upon her. It was not to be endured; crimsoning with annoyance, Laura sprang to her feet, exclaiming haughtily:

"Well, Miss Renwick, may I ask why I am favored with your flattering attention?"

Surprised at this sudden outbreak, Mary drew back, and half-doubting if the challenging tone was intended to be taken seriously, said with good-humored archness:

"I beg your pardon; yet even Grimalkin may blink at a king, you know."

"Spare me your witticisms, if you please; I fear I am not clever enough to appreciate them," rejoined Laura tartly; "but I would give a penny for your thoughts, since you have done me the honor of staring at me for fully five minutes by the clock."

Mary lost patience.

"Would you really like to know of what I was thinking?"

Laura nodded. "I am going to have my mental and moral photograph presented in no very attractive manner," she said to herself, "but I have always felt matters would end in an open quarrel with this girl and it has come at last."

"Laura Gaines, you have always been mean and disagreeable to me," began Mary hotly, "and you seem to think me as ungenerous and spiteful as yourself—but if you *must* know what was in my mind while I was watching you—"

"Yes?"

"Well—I was thinking—Laura does not like me—one could not call her amiable—but how pretty she is—how charming to look at! As pretty as the lovely French doll I was so fond of when I was a child; how proud her father must be of her!"

This reply was jerked out abruptly, but had the floor opened, or the ceiling fallen, Laura would not have been more surprised. The glow in her cheeks deepened until they were red as a peony, and she started back as if she had been stung. Mary, however, was too angry to pay any heed; hastily putting away her books, she slammed down the cover of her desk and was about to leave the room when she was arrested by a curt:

"Wait a moment, please."

Something in the tone caused her to hesitate. Her intention had certainly not been to conciliate Laura; on the contrary, she had been actuated principally by offended pride, and a wish to prove that *she* was above the petty malice shown by her schoolmates. Hardly the soft answer which turneth away wrath, but rather the flaring up of a little electric spark. The retort, however, flashed a sudden light into the consciousness of the listener. The revelation was far from pleasant notwithstanding, and did not improve matters, for the unexpected speech sounded ironical to Laura; to realize a fault is one thing, to calmly submit to the satirical heaping of coals of fire upon one's head is quite another.

"Wait a moment," she repeated, and then went on impetuously, as Mary wheeled around and stood regarding her: " I dare say you are right; no doubt I deserve to be stared at as though I were a doll, Miss Renwick; no doubt my father is proud to have a doll for a daughter!"

"But I did not mean any sarcasm," protested Mary, seeing that her words had been misconstrued; "I—I am sorry I spoke."

Laura experienced another revulsion of feeling. Mary had been sincere, then; the words at which she had taken offence were not intended as a taunt. And did she really look passably well in this old frock without a bit of style to it? Why, if so,—the discovery was so astounding that her surprise seemed to concentrate into one big exclamation-point,—why, then, style and dress were not everything after all; one might be really attractive, and even admired, without them.

"Yet as to papa being proud of me," she reflected, with bitter self-reproach; "how could he be, indeed, when I have shown about as much feeling or consideration for him as a doll, anyhow? Less in fact, for a doll always has a smiling face at least, and how cross I have been at home during the last few days, when poor papa has so much to worry him. Well, well, I shall try to show him I am not so heartless as I have seemed. Mary must be a nice girl, as Tessie said, for with every reason for dislike she was thinking kindly of me. I am sure I should never be so generous as to indulge in any complimentary speculations regarding any one who acted to me as I have towards her."

The changes of expression in Laura's face revealed something of what was passing in her mind, and presently in a softened manner she said aloud: "I have been horrid to you, Mary, ever since you came to school here. I wish I could make you forget it!"

"Oh, do not say any more," entreated Mary, shrinking with shy awkwardness from the apology: "I—I must be going home—" and catching up her jacket and hat she fled precipitately, almost running against Miss Langdon, who was just entering the room.

"Ah, my dear, you are ready for me I presume," said Madame, appearing not to notice Laura's flushed countenance and embarrassed demeanor; "I am glad you and Mary Renwick have been chatting together; the sound of your voices reached me as I came along the corridor. I have noted with chagrin and dissatisfaction that some of your classmates have not been friendly to this gentle little new scholar;—such petty jealousy is unworthy of my girls. I am personally much interested in Mary; her mother was the beauty of our school in Paris, and of high social connections. Her father is greatly respected; the son of a wealthy New York capitalist, he chose, in a financial crisis, to sacrifice his own fortune rather than cause severe loss to those who trusted in him. I was happy when he brought his daughter to me saying he now found himself able to provide for her education. You see my young friend comes naturally by her refinement and nobility of character and I trust her companions will soon learn to appreciate her."

Laura mumbled a half-incoherent reply, and handing Madame the book of the play, plunged into the recitation of her lines.

"Only fancy!" she said later, when recounting the incident to Tessie; "and we thought Mary Renwick was a little nobody! I suppose when the girls hear her story they will regret having slighted her in such a snobbish manner."

"For my part," answered Tessie; "I am still more ashamed that we treated her so ill-naturedly when we thought she was merely a protégée of Madame's; for under those circumstances we should have been especially kind to her."

CHAPTER VIII.

MOTHER'S WELCOME HOME.

AT last the joyful news came to the Marrons that grandfather had almost recovered from his recent illness, and, after the many delays and disappointments, mother was really coming home. What a fever of excitement they were all in, as the hour of her expected arrival drew near! Father and the boys went to the railway station to meet her, but, notwithstanding this partition of the family enthusiasm into instalments, when the carriage drew up before the front gate what a commotion there was, as the girls made a rush for the first glimpse of her sweet face.

Before papa had a chance to assist her to alight May and Toosie had tumbled into the coach, each eager for the first kiss; a moment afterwards Tessie's arms were around her and thus, encompassed by love and caresses, the dear mother was conducted in triumph up the walk to the front door, where Delia, her honest countenance beaming with an expansive smile, stood crying:

"Oh, but it's a blessed day that brings you back to your own again, ma'am! And a gladsome sight to behold you looking so well! Sure, it's long you have been away from us!"

"Yes, indeed, and very happy I am to be at home once more," answered Mrs. Marron, warmly returning her affectionate handclasp.

Chuckling with satisfaction Delia hastened away to serve up such a dinner as "the mistress" declared she had not seen surpassed in point of cookery even at the Fifth Avenue Hotel where she had been staying with her father. Meantime the boys, who, grinning with delight, had witnessed the enthusiasm of the welcome from the box of the hack, scrambled down, sportively disputed with father for the honor of carrying in the traveller's satchel and shawl-strap, and wrested them from him while he was giving directions about the trunk.

In the sitting-room, mother having kissed May and Toosie again, drew Tessie to her heart in a fond embrace saying with emotion: "My precious daughter, what a help and treasure you have been to me!" an expression of affection which compensated the joyous girl a thousand times for all the small annoyances of the past long, tedious weeks.

Such was the happy home-coming.

And what souvenirs mother brought for each and every one of the household. "It was like having Christmas over again," the children declared. For there were not only the gifts from herself, but others from grandfather and Aunt Emily; till, as Delia averred, "the skies ac'tially seemed to rain presents; and sure, it would take a year and a day to tell them all!"

Tessie received, with many "ohs" and "ahs" of admiration and pleasure, the beautiful Venetian necklace, and the gloves from Paris that fell to her share; but perhaps she was never more touched and pleased in her life than when Mrs. Marron drew from many wrappings of paper a roll of shimmering fabric, that shaded in the loveliest way from heliotrope to violet, and, playfully casting a fold of the silken material about her daughter's shoulders, said:

"My dear, I appreciated your little sacrifice in wearing the crimson frock as it was, to Laura's party, and, therefore, knowing how a girl longs for her first silk frock and also the pleasure she takes in it, I have brought you this."

"Oh, mother, mother, how good you are!" was all the delighted girl could say, but she embraced the little woman ecstatically and then buried her face in the soft silk.

Of course she must at once see the effect in the mirror; but as she contemplated the pretty apparition therein reflected, her smile faded, and turning around abruptly, she exclaimed:

"It is awfully selfish of me to be so jubilant over the possession of this exquisite stuff. I cannot feel sorry you got it, yet I really do wish, mother, you had bought instead the black silk gown you have needed so long. It is a shame you should go without that gown just to deck out in gay plumage such a vain little peacock as I am."

Mrs. Marron laughed merrily, but her eyes were suspiciously misty as she said, patting the hands that were impulsively laid upon her own: "Thank you for your thoughtfulness, love. You may, however, enjoy your simple silk frock to your heart's content without fear of selfishness, for when Aunt Emily went away your father entrusted to her a commission without my knowledge, and the result is a Paris gown almost too splendid for a quiet little woman like me."

"O mother! how grand! No; nothing is too splendid for you," broke in Tessie, now entirely happy. "Is it in your trunk? I am all impatience to see it!"

* * * *

Tessie remained at home from Miss Langdon's for several days after her mother's return. When she finally went back to school she was, of course, primed with innumerable subjects to be talked over with Laura. There were not only the presents to be described; Mrs. Marron's visit to New York, as well as grandfather's and Aunt Emily's tour abroad.

had to be dwelt upon, and many interesting stories of travel to be repeated.

"Dear me, what a glorious time you have had!" commented Laura, as though her friend had been the chief actor in it all. "It really seems an age since you were here. Nothing of interest has happened, but—yes, I have one piece of news for you. We are to have another new scholar—some one quite out of the ordinary—in fact no less a personage than a real, live Marchésa."

"What is a Marchésa?" demanded Tessie stupidly, "a mummy or a monkey, or—"

"Nonsense! Think a moment and you will recollect. A Marchésa is a noble Italian lady, in rank above a countess."

"A lady of exalted rank in Perryville? Where on earth did she come from?"

"From some part of Italy, as you might have inferred," replied Laura facetiously.

"I understand; coronets and titles are as numerous over there as blackberries in midsummer. But how did she hear of *our* school?"

"Through some lady who was a schoolmate of Miss Langdon's in Paris; the daughters of half the notabilities of the age must have been educated at that famous convent, to judge from the romantic histories we sometimes get an inkling of, and the interesting personalities of Madame's acquaintance."

"And so a genuine Marchésa is coming to

school with plain American girls!" mused Tessie aloud.

"*Plain*, indeed!" echoed Laura mockingly, glancing around for a mirror.

"Laura, do not be absurd! You know I intended it in the sense of untitled."

"Well, every American girl is noble in her own right."

"Stuff! But what does it mean at all, at all, as Delia says? Why is she in the United States?"

"Who, Delia? Because her people thought this a better country to get along in than their own."

"No, stupid; I referred to the Countess."

"For much the same reason, doubtless: namely, that the family exchequer is sadly depleted, and her ladyship's mamma hopes to refill it upon this side of the Atlantic."

"Still, you have given me no decided information."

Laura opened her eyes very wide: "No decided information!" she repeated, "when I assure you that you are to have so distinguished a schoolmate!"

"Nonsense!" replied Tessie, with an independent shrug of the shoulders. "Some one has been hoaxing you; presently you will discover the pretensions of the young lady to be a farce."

"Not at all. Mr. Belotti is my authority;

he descanted upon the theme in the pauses of my singing-lesson this morning."

"Did he say why she is coming here?"

"To study, and recite if she can, *cher petit choux;* to be nagged by Miss Carstens, awe-struck by the perfections of Mary Renwick, and impressed by the *grande manière* of Madame."

"No, but, seriously—"

"Well, then, Mlle. Ingénue, it appears that her mother, a rather dashing widow, and also a titled lady of course, has been creating quite a sensation among the fashionable set in New York and elsewhere, and one of our nabobs is going to marry her. Under these circumstances, mamma finds the Marchésa a trifle in the way, and has arranged to have her come to Miss Langdon for a while upon the plea of improving her knowledge of English. When the date of the marriage is decided no doubt la Signorina will be invited home to give her consent."

"Laura, you ridiculous girl—"

"Are you satisfied now?"

"Yes, and curious, I must admit."

"Your curiosity shall soon be appeased; she is expected to-morrow."

Thanks perhaps to Professor Belotti's reportorial abilities, the intelligence had already spread through the school and the new arrival was anticipated with either amused or eager interest.

"What do you suppose the Marchésa will be like?" asked little May Marron, as she tripped homeward beside Tessie and her friends.

"Like Golden Hair, when she struck the three bears dumb with admiration," hazarded Emily Carrington.

"Or else decked out in white satin and jewels, like Cinderella going to the ball," surmised Laura.

"Only possibly she may wear a gold coronet instead of a hat," added Irene.

"Oh, oh!" ejaculated the little maid in round-eyed wonder, making up her mind to be on hand for the first glimpse of the stranger.

If the older pupils had no such extravagant anticipations, nevertheless, with few exceptions, each in imagination limned for herself a more or less pleasing picture of the expected new scholar, and several even quietly resolved to cultivate the friendship of the Marchésa without delay.

"Of course she will be beautiful, or at least of distinguished manners and bearing," said Emily, with an air which might lead one to suppose she had spent her life mainly in the society of illustrious personages.

"I am just dying to see her frocks," owned Laura; "the Professor mentioned incidentally that she spent the autumn in Paris."

"Ah, we shall be sure to obtain the latest

styles from her, then," continued Irene; "as she is to board here, Miss Langdon has had the blue room at the head of the stairs prepared for her. I hope she will find the lovely nook, with its chintz-covered furniture and pretty lace curtains, suited to her taste."

The next afternoon during recreation a carriage rattled up the street and came to a stop before the old mansion. Little May spied it from one of the windows, and the news quickly reached the other pupils, who were promenading in the long corridor or gallery.

What more natural than that several, audacious enough to brave Miss Langdon's reproving frown, should saunter towards the front hall to witness the reception? Annette, the white-capped, bright-eyed mulatto waitress, opened the door, and extended her small silver tray for the cards of the visitors, but it was the coachman who brushed past her, almost knocking the tray from her hand, and depositing various pieces of luggage in the middle of the floor. Then there swept by a tall, handsome woman, whom Annette ushered into the parlor.

"The mother," whispered Laura to Irene, in the recess of a window, where they had paused as if by chance.

The handsome woman was followed by an overgrown, awkward figure.

"Her maid?" conjectured Irene; "now for our Signorina herself."

But no one else followed, and Annette shut the hall door with a bang, making a grimace at the coachman behind it. The two girls exchanged glances. Could that gawky creature in the dowdy frock, ill-fitting jacket, cotton gloves, and a hat of last year's mode be the Marchésa?

Whatever doubts they might have entertained upon the subject were speedily terminated, however, for the older lady soon went away again in the carriage, and presently Miss Langdon came out of the parlor with the young stranger, and introduced her to the pupils as Miss Olivia Parmesano. Nevertheless, before they could make much progress towards acquaintance, the bell rang for afternoon class, and Miss Parmesano was conducted to her room by Annette, in order that she might rest after her journey from New York and dispose her belongings.

On the way back to the study room the older girls encountered little May curled up on one of the broad window-ledges of the corridor, and shedding tears of vexation.

"You mean cheats, to tell me such a string of nonsense!" cried the child.

"Well, how did I know how a Marchésa would look? I never saw one before, either," said Irene, laughing.

"I do not believe she is a real Marchésa at all," grumbled May.

"Oh, yes, she is; I heard Miss Langdon say so to Miss Carstens," maintained Emily.

"But Madame called her Miss Parmesano."

"Because she is supposed to be among us incognito," ventured Laura facetiously.

May looked properly impressed; the idea of the incognito appealed to her fancy, and consoled her for the discovery that the Marchésa was only an unprepossessing, overgrown girl, after all.

CHAPTER IX.

SIGNORINA AND PRINCESS.

No chatelaine who ever graced an ancestral hall was animated by a prouder, haughtier spirit than Miss Olivia Parmesano, Marchésa di Niente, or "Livvy," as a number of her schoolmates insisted upon calling her.

"Her ladyship need not think she is going to rule over us," asserted Laura, discussing the newcomer with her friends. "If she does not intend to treat us with due respect, she may anticipate being paid back in her own coin."

"Miss Langdon told me once that a princess who was at school with her in Paris was the most gentle and considerate for others of all the pupils," volunteered Tessie.

"Yes, Madame says Olivia is simply spoiled, and we ought to prove to her, by our own unfailing politeness, that the true American lady needs no patent of nobility. Or better still, that the courtesy of the Catholic girl and woman should be modelled upon the imitation of Our Blessed Lady," suggested Mary Renwick with diffidence.

The words did not fail of their effect, although Emily Carrington hastened to bridge over the momentary pause, observing in her dry, humorous way:

"Oh, well, my mother does not send me here to teach the Marchésa how to behave, and la Signorina (or whatever they call her in la bella Italia) had better mend her manners—else my resolutions to be forbearing and all the rest will be broken almost as fast as I can make them. I do hope the marriage of the widow and the nabob will come off soon, so Livvy may be spirited away to Europe again; for no doubt, being a nabob, her prospective stepfather affects to consider this country hardly interesting enough to live in for long at a time."

Ungainly and awkward, with sallow complexion, expressionless black eyes, and a mop of curly dark hair hanging about her shoulders, Olivia, notwithstanding her plain appearance and homely gowns, exerted a kind of influence among the girls—an influence that differed in accordance with their own dispositions and characters.

To Laura she was another revelation that modish frocks do not always constitute the principal claim to distinction, even in fashionable society. To others she was always the Marchésa, and they either stood a little in awe of her or strove to be on good terms with her accordingly; the more independent, like Tessie and Emily, merely laughed at her queer ways and resented her assumption of superiority, while quiet Mary Renwick found her a curious study; for to Mary (who had spent so much of her short life without young friends), the companions of her school-days still possessed something of the interest of story-book heroines.

But Miss Parmesano, as she was called by her teachers, contracted no particular friendships and held aloof from all as far as possible. Meantime the reputation of Miss Langdon's school increased, and she began to have more applications than she could accept from parents who wished to place their daughters with her as boarding pupils. One day, late in the winter, another singular personality appeared upon the scene.

It was the hour of recreation, and the pupils were promenading by threes and fours in the garden of the old mansion. Suddenly Madame came out of the house. Her long cloak, and the scarf of black lace which she had hastily donned as a head-covering, gave her a madonna or nun-like appearance; but the young people scarcely noticed what a charming picture she made, so engrossed was their attention by the apparition at her side.

"Is this an Eskimo I see before me?" apostrophized Emily in mingled amusement and astonishment. "Who shall we have here next? For a *select* school the selection of pupils in this establishment is assuredly most extraordinary!"

The young person who accompanied Madame was enveloped in a coat of gray astrakhan, and wore a cap of the same fur. She was straight as an arrow, and her black hair fell on her neck—not in a bushy mass like Olivia's, but in straggling locks, which clever, sharp-tongued Emily compared to the serpent tresses of Medusa. The newcomer was good-looking, nevertheless, with bright hazel eyes, and a brunette complexion, that now, in the girl's excitement at meeting so many strangers, deepened to a rich, warm tint.

"An Indian, as we are alive!" exclaimed Laura; "a composite of Pocahontas, Minnehaha, and the rest!" It was a real disappointment when they caught her name as Madame repeated it to Miss Carstens, the teacher in charge.

"Eva Thompson? How commonplace! I expected it would be something as musical as Coaina, at least," said Tessie.

When, after their walk in the fresh, clear air, the bevy of girls returned to the study-room, many curious eyes wandered in the direction of the new scholar, to note how she appeared divested of her polar wrap. Another sensation was the result, for the attire of the unique Miss Thompson was a study in color that would have delighted the soul of an artist, but was, as Emily expressed it, "rather too striking outside of a picture frame." The gaudy frock and the yellow ribbon that kept the elf-like locks back from her intense face were odd enough, but strangest of all was the string of amber beads, each twice the size of a pea, which she wore tightly clasped about her dark but well-formed throat.

The young stranger was manifestly indebted to the race of Minnehaha for the singular beauty which her critics, diverted by her fantastic apparel, in no wise appreciated.

"What a guy!" giggled Emily to Tessie.

"Oh, don't!" begged the latter. "You know we agreed at the last meeting of our 'Gentle Words Society' not to make derogatory remarks about our neighbors."

Before the close of the day Eva was as much at home as though she had been a boarder at Miss Langdon's since the school opened. By no means afflicted with shyness, and pleased to be the centre of attraction, she told her history unreservedly.

"My mother," she said, "was an Indian girl named Gentle Fawn, who, having been sent to school in the East, returned to her people as a teacher. Gentle Fawn was very pretty, and soon after her return she was married to a brave and good paleface, a young agent of the Government at the reservation. I do not remember her, for she died when I was very young, but my father and I have always been devoted to each other."

This romantic story was received, of course, with much interest. Encouraged by the rapt attention with which her auditors hung upon her words, Eva, only stopping to draw breath, proceeded to embellish and add to the facts in a manner which certainly contributed greatly to the picturesqueness of the narrative; and although several among her listeners shrugged their shoulders and looked incredulous, others accepted the tale in all seriousness, at least for the nonce.

"When I was still a small child," she ran on, "there was trouble at the reservation and a whole band of Indians took their departure, going far into the wilds. Before long my nurse, an old squaw, stole after them, taking me with her. I can just recollect that she carried me strapped on her shoulders like a pappoose, around the mountain, by wood and ravine, across stream and torrent, to the encampment of the disaffected tribe, who welcomed her with joy and chose me as their queen—for my mother was the granddaughter of one of their famous chiefs."

"Great Scott! Another lady of exalted rank!" ejaculated Laura, in an aside to Tessie; "after a while it will be a novelty to find a girl in this school who has not a title of distinction—"

"Pocahontas was not a circumstance to this gentle savage, it appears. Oh, for a lodge in some vast wilderness, a mat of rushes and a pair of moccasins!" interjected the irrepressible Emily.

"And did you really stay there and rule over the Indians?" asked little May Marron of the stranger, whom she had been regarding with round-eyed wonder.

"Yes, for two years, until my father found me and carried me home with him. He had to regain possession of me by stratagem, and when they discovered that their Queen had been made away with there was a rumpus, I can tell you; a regular outbreak that extended to other tribes, and the military had to be called out to put them down."

"What is the word for Eva in the Indian language?" inquired May, properly impressed.

"Fudge, Miss Simplicity! My name among them was not Eva, but—" for the first time the narrator paused. Was it her inventive faculty or merely her memory that momentarily failed? Or did she fear, perhaps, that the revelation might destroy her quickly acquired prestige? "Well," she added presently with a laugh, "my name among them was Wopsiewahwah."

"Hurrah for Wopsie!" cried mischievous May, dancing down the room.

The cheer was taken up by the lively older girls, and thus, amid merriment and applause, Wopsie made her entrance into school-life at Miss Langdon'r

CHAPTER X.

AN ABORIGINAL CELEBRATION.

To the majority of the girls Wopsie's pretensions were a huge joke, but chief among those who regarded them seriously was, strangely enough, the haughty Olivia.

"Did you ever!" said Emily Carrington to Laura one day: "it is the best comedy on record; la Marchésa has taken up with Pocahontas in dead earnest as the only one in the school whose social rank approaches her own. Is it not ridiculous?"

"Oh, of course! they stand upon a higher plane than the rest of the world," responded Laura ironically. "But surely our royal aborigine has the advantage, for, while Olivia claims to be merely a marchioness, Wopsie, according to her own account, is a crowned queen."

In truth Olivia had unbent wonderfully towards the stranger from the Far West. Before she came to the United States her notions of America and Americans had been very vague. Once, during her early days at Miss Langdon's, the geography class was nearly convulsed with laughter over her announcement that San Francisco was a suburb of Chicago; another time she inquired with some concern if the bears and buffaloes ever came out of the woods in the vicinity of Perryville and walked about the town.

She had supposed the Indians still formed a considerable proportion of the population of the country, and the discovery that the small "remnant of the mighty race" now remaining lived apart, on reservations, only gave a more decided form to her admiration of them. "Attila" was her favorite romance, and she had stumbled through portions of the musical verse of the story of Minnehaha, in reading English with her governess. Consequently when Wopsie, the living representative of these beautiful daughters of the forest, appeared upon the commonplace scene of her Perryville surroundings, Olivia congratulated herself, for Wopsie, she decided, was best fitted to be her companion.

The two girls were soon upon the best of terms, both being boarders at the school. No one, however, was more amused than Wopsie at Olivia's respect for her supposed rank among the semi-civilized and wandering people she had known in early childhood.

The Marchésa would fain have kept her chosen associate all to herself.

"I pray you make not friends with zese nobodies, you who are true American of ze old race," she urged. "To make companion of zem is not for your dignity nor mine. We be together, we two, by descent and nature, apart from all ze rest."

This was too much for Wopsie, who silently shook with laughter.

"Ees eet not so?" demanded Olivia peremptorily.

"Oh, yes, to be sure, I like to have you for my friend," Wopsie answered as soon as she could trust herself to speak. "But, you see, a little over a hundred years ago the Declaration of Independence pronounced all the people of this country free and equal. Being a foreigner, *you* may act as you please, but it would never do for me to be too exclusive."

So *la damina di qualitá* was forced to resign herself to what she was pleased to designate the requirements of Wopsie's position as an American princess in this degenerate age.

"Livvy is immensely entertaining when she gets upon her high horse of *noblesse oblige*," Wopsie confided to Tessie Marron. "It is as good as the minstrels, or a stage farce, to hear her. But at other times it is a bit dull to go with her altogether." And quiet and dulness being what Wopsie most abhorred, she soon became a leader in all the school larks and escapades.

* * * *

It was now February, and the next Wednesday would be Washington's Birthday. Miss Langdon had announced that the pupils might spend the day at the school and have *congé*, or, in plain English, the freedom of the dear old house, with permission to make as merry as they pleased. Tessie and several of her friends stood in the long corridor discussing various plans for the celebration of the day.

"We might get up charades," proposed Laura, whose spirits had revived of late since her father's affairs had begun to look brighter, and there was every indication that he would be able to extricate himself from his financial difficulties.

"Or it would be great sport to play *cache cache*, hide-and-seek, with the players divided into two bands or parties, you know," said Emily.

"Yes, only in that case there would be such a hubbub and commotion, Madame might fancy a band of wild Indians had come to steal Wopsie away again," objected Mary Renwick, with a laugh.

"Well, charades would be entertaining," pronounced Tessie.

"I'll tell you what would be grand!" cried Wopsie herself, coming up at that moment. "Suppose we present a picture of American life in the early days of the Colonies; didn't I hear somebody mention Indians, just now?"

The girls looked disconcerted, but no one replied.

"Yes, we must have Indians; it would be so interesting for la Marchésa, for instance."

Wopsie's eyes sparkled as the notion unfolded itself to her fertile fancy. Plotting innocent mischief was her specialty.

"What do *you* say?" queried Emily, after they had gayly agreed to consider any plan she might favor or bring forward, provided it was not too wild or extravagant.

"Oh, I don't know— Let me think. As it will be a national holiday, we ought to commemorate an incident in United States history, and thus introduce the aborigines."

There was a short pause, during which the girls set their wits to work.

"I have it!" suddenly concluded Wopsie jubilantly, but almost in a whisper. "There was the Boston Tea Party, where the patriots, disguised as Indians, forced their way into the English ships and threw overboard the cargo of taxed tea. Suppose we give a reception after the same style? Those staid worthies have been glorified ever since for their cleverness in imposing upon the domineering foreigner; why should we not follow their example?"

"Oh, Wopsie, you are too ridiculous!" laughed Tessie, in the same low tone. "The project is a splendid one, however, for in addition to the opportunity it offers to impress la Signorina it will admit of our entertaining the whole school by a novel afternoon tea."

"It would certainly add to the *éclat* to have refreshments," said Laura.

"Yes, yes, let us serve tea in dainty little cups, and have cake," seconded Emily.

"And doughnuts—that toothsome Colonial delicacy which has never gone out of fashion, among girls and boys, anyhow," added Tessie. "Delia makes delicious doughnuts, and I have learned how to cook them myself, too; I can promise to bring a good-sized basketful."

"Do, then," rejoined Wopsie ecstatically.

A conference ensued upon the edibles, china, etc., to be provided, each girl agreeing to furnish something for the feast.

"But we must keep the plan a complete secret," cautioned Wopsie, "otherwise half of the fun would be lost. To-morrow after school come to my room; you know it is on the floor above Livvy's and quite out of the way. We will there decide about our costumes and settle all details."

"Grand! Mum's the word!" cried Irene Wier, with her finger on her lips.

The others imitated the gesture in token of the bond between them; forthwith they tiptoed to the clothes-press, secured their jackets and hats and went quietly home; all but Wopsie, who shut herself in her own room to ransack her bureau for articles or trinkets that might be available for the project. For several days following the plotters were quietly busied, and, it must be admitted, found some difficulty in keeping their minds on their lessons during the hours of study and class.

* * * *

On the morning of Washington's Birthday the sun rose gloriously, as if willing to do all in its power to enhance the brilliancy of the national celebration. It was a perfect winter's day, the air being crisp, clear, and cold, and although there was no snow on the ground, the Marron boys, who made an early excursion to the lake, reported the skating all that could be desired.

But the novelty of spending a part of the holiday at Miss Langdon's proved the chief attraction for the majority of her pupils. Betimes in the afternoon they gathered in the old mansion, accordingly, and, amid games, dancing, and romping, merriment reigned supreme. The rumor that there was to be a play, or at least some kind of dramatic representation, added the pleasure of anticipation to their enjoyment. No one knew exactly what it was to be, the little air of mystery was very fascinating, and curiosity was soon wrought up to the highest pitch. Even the usually indifferent Olivia became excited and impatient for the coming disclosure.

"Wopsiewahwah has to me a degree of ze scheme unfolded," she condescended to inform Mary Renwick, who, having been absent a day or two and, consequently, unable to attend rehearsals, had been obliged to resign her part in the program.

Mary smiled and asked: "Are you quite sure? Perhaps it was only a pretence."

"Wopsiewahwah would with me pretend never," returned the Marchésa haughtily. "No; it ees—there can no harm be in saying now—it ees zat she ees to present as a picture 'er life before she came here, ze life you all 'ave in America lived one 'undred year ago."

Mary, turning away, buried her face in her handkerchief to hide her amusement. Presently came the tinkle of the school-bell, so often heard with reluctance, but now so welcome. In response to its summons the girls, large and small, thronged to the study-room.

But what a transformation had been here effected! The desks had vanished, and in their place was a young forest of fir-trees that, like Aladdin's palace, seemed to have sprung up in the night. Soft music floated on the air. The scene was lighted solely by the dim red glow of a camp-fire burning before the door of a picturesque wigwam hung with buffalo-skins and mats.

Breaking into a chorus of delighted "ohs," the spectators pressed forward, but soon found their progress interrupted by a rope barrier stretched across the room. Mary kept close to Olivia, wishing to have the full benefit of her impressions. "I must this well note for the book I will one day about America write," she stated gravely. While she spoke the music changed to a minor key, and took on an element of wildness; there was a rustling noise at the farther end of the room, and straightway from ambush sprang a band of menacing Indians, brandishing tomahawks, and glaring fiercely at the assembly. The younger spectators screamed and there was a stampede for the door; several of the older girls also beat a hasty retreat.

The desired sensation having been created, however, the order of exercises was all at once changed. The harmonies grew glad again as the singing of birds in primeval woods, and a voice that sounded like Emily's said reassuringly:

"Friends and allies, you have nothing to fear. Come forward again, therefore, and the beautiful Iroquois maiden, Irenehaha, will pass the pipe of peace."

Thereupon stepped forth from the semi-darkness into the light of the fire a tattooed damsel, clad in a motley-colored tunic and skirt, with a scarlet blanket draped from her shoulders. An enormous feather head-dress and large hooped earrings completed her adornment. In her left hand she carried an adobe bowl, while her right held a pipe with a stem a yard long.

"*Una pipa!*" murmured the Signorina; "ze cigaretta I know—yes—in my country some ladies—well, zey a little cigaretta *puff,*

puff, perhaps; but ees eet indeed true zat your grandmozzers did ze pipa smoke?"

"No, no," protested Mary, with a horrified laugh. "Wait and you will see."

Meantime the mysterious voice, that proceeded apparently from the heart of the wood, continued:

"Yes, Irenehaha will pass the pipe of peace, but, as a concession to the prejudices of the fair palefaces against the smoking 'of the herbs and leaves of fragrance, the tobacco from the South land,' be it known the pipes are intended only *for the blowing of soap bubbles*. Many pipes will be passed, and whoever blows the largest bubble from this foaming bowl shall be most pleasing in the eyes of our Queen Wopsiewahwah!"

There was a general giggle; only Olivia preserved her gravity, half believing that the audience were invited to take part in some aboriginal rite.

"Ugh!" responded Irenehaha, proceeding to distribute the pipes with solemn formality. The light from the chandeliers now flashed upon the scene, and the fun began in earnest; there arose a babel of merry voices, with moments of silence as each of the company strove to blow the greatest bubble, warning off her companions with emphatically imploring gestures, and watching with admiration the airy sphere expanding and scintillating at the end of her pipe, or floating away, too soon, alas, to fade into nothingness. And all the while, dumb and imperturbable, the strange Iroquois maiden moved here and there, noting all, and blowing by far the most beautiful bubbles herself. At last, shaking with suppressed mirth, she paused before Olivia, who had not taken part in the scramble.

"Oh, ha!" cried the Marchésa, peering into the dusky face: "Irene, eet ees indeed! Ah, ah, very clever, of a truth; was eet so your grandmozzer she look? As for ze blow—I know not if I can." She accepted the pipe, however. "*Puff, puff*—ah, eet ees not like to ze cigaretta."

"No," agreed Irenehaha laconically, but with twinkling eyes.

The Signorina made one or two more ludicrous attempts.

"Ah, non!" she repeated, throwing away the pipe, "ze Europeana ees not to ze manner born, as your Shakespeare say."

After much active competition, small May Marron was declared the victor in the soap-bubble contest.

Now the lights grew dim again and even the red glimmer of the camp-fire died down so that the room was left almost in darkness.

"What are you going to do?" demanded the girls. But even as they spoke it grew bright, this time revealing the interior of the wigwam, with Queen Wopsie seated upon a low couch purporting to be covered with buffalo-skins — although a nearer inspection would have revealed sundry familiar seal coats and capes. The flowing tresses of the dusky princess were, like those of Irenehaha, crowned with a formidable array of feathers. She wore a parti-colored costume, which gradually resolved itself into a sky-blue dressing-gown, a plaided shawl, and a yellow table-cover. About her neck was twined in many rows a long string of crystal beads, and upon her feet were elaborately embroidered moccasins. The savage beauty of her dark features was heightened by the dash of carmine upon cheeks and lips; in short she fully realized Olivia's ideal of an untutored daughter of the forest.

By a royal gesture of command, the queen signed to little May to take the place near her on the divan, saying: "It is meet you should sit beside me, for you also are a queen, and reign supreme in the fairyland of bubbles."

The child shrank back with half-timorous, half-amused reluctance, however; Wopsie did not press the point, but, turning to a second attendant who appeared at this moment from among the firs, the Indian princess continued with a wave of the hand:

"Emiliwanda, explain to our friends and allies the nature of the celebration which they have honored with their presence."

Emiliwanda advanced. The details of her attire comprised all the bright shades known to the dyer's art, upon a foundation of orange-colored flannel; her necklace was of shells and alligator's teeth; over her shoulder was slung a quiver of arrows, and she carried a bow, like a typical Indian amazon. Mounting a chair, she began to declaim upon the subject of the Boston Tea Party, keeping her eyes fixed on Olivia the while, and in her eloquence quite surpassing all previous orators, and beggaring the descriptions of all former historians or romance writers—at least so said the audience, who listened with breathless attention and at the close broke into tumultuous applause.

Emiliwanda bowed low, and withdrew. Wopsiewahwah again waved her hand: "Tessiekee and Lauraqua," cried she, "attend to the entertainment of our guests."

Immediately a third Indian attendant appeared, bearing a tray of dainty cups of tea; and after her came still another carrying a basket piled high with golden doughnuts, which she deftly passed and then flitted away, to return anon with cookies and candies. The gas-jets were turned up full blaze, and the guests ventured nearer, convinced that the *belle sauvage* who provided such delectable refection must be amicably disposed towards them. The rope barrier was broken down, and gradually the bronze-red faces of the bizarre queen and her companions became

less strange. Beneath the coloring of burnt
sienna and the lavish prinking with more
garish pigments the spectators were able to
recognize not only the familiar lineaments of
Wopsie, but the features of Irene, Laura,
Tessie, and Emily. And none seemed to appreciate and enjoy it all more than Olivia,
Marchésa di Niente. She studied the costumes,
toyed with the baubles worn by the Indian
maidens, and was delighted with the wigwam
—even although a closer view revealed it to be
but a clever combination of commonplace
window draperies, mats, and fur rugs.

Unfortunately the best of good times must
come to an end. All too soon the old clock in
the hall struck six, and the party broke up
after thanking their strange hostesses for the
diversions of the afternoon. La Signorina
was the last to offer her congratulations.

"Eet was charming indeed," she affirmed,
with condescending graciousness. "And I am
to you indebted for this so true picture of ze
early American life and manners. So thus
eet was you people here did live one 'undred
year ago? Ze dress ees festive, and ze little
dough cakes are not bad; more sweet zan ze
tortillas of ze Mexican for an instance. I
will put zem, ze toothsome littler dough cakes,
in my book."

But ere she could say more the Indians
dashed precipitately away, and possibly the
hilarious outbreak which presently awoke the

echoes of the corridor was also set down in the Signorina's chronicle of the wonderful experiences of her sojourn in the United States.

"What absurdity ees eet now? Zese Americana, 'ave zey—what ees ze name?—ah, yes—'ave zey ze 'ighstricks [hysterics]?" she soliloquized, and betook herself to the seclusion of the little blue nook above the hall door, where she could reflect undisturbed over the events of the day.

"What fun, girls!" cried Wopsie, as soon as she could speak for laughing. "Who ever imagined that Livvy would take our masquerading all in earnest? I thought she would see the hoax at once and join in the sport. Oh, dear, oh, dear! Well, anyhow, our American Tea Party has been a success from beginning to end."

CHAPTER XI.

THE LITERARY CLUB.

It was not long, however, ere Olivia discovered the true nature of the Washington Birthday celebration, and, aroused at what she was pleased to consider a special indignity to herself, her resentment was extreme, especially against Wopsie.

"And you, mees," she almost screamed, after an exhibition of temper as much beyond the average of schoolgirl petulance as was her assumption of superiority above their claim to social distinction—"you 'ave forfeit my regard forever. I credit not you are a real princess; you are but like ze ozzers."

"Thanks," retaliated Wopsie, sarcastically. "I have never been so proud as to wish to look down on others, and I am quite willing to leave you alone in your glory. So, *addio* and *buona fortuna*, Signorina."

"Farewell, a long farewell to all my greatness," she ejaculated a few moments later, shutting herself into her own room.

And yet, presently, as she flitted about, flourishing a feather duster that had been robbed to eke out the plumage of the Indian head-dresses, her smile grew a trifle bitter. For Wopsie was conscious that, although considered a lively companion during recreation hours, she was not genuinely a favorite with all of her schoolmates.

"Pshaw!" she continued to herself; "I do not care a straw for Olivia's affected superiority, but I do want to be popular, and to be esteemed one of the cleverest girls of the school!"

Of her cleverness there could be no doubt. She now contested closely with Tessie Marron and Mary Renwick for the honors of Miss Carstens' class. But it was not the ambition to attain first rank so much as an idle vanity, an overanxiety to attract attention for the moment, to surprise by a meteor-like brilliancy rather than to shine steadily as a star of the first magnitude in the firmament of school-life, that was to be poor Wopsie's undoing.

The Literary Club was a social organization among the girls at Miss Langdon's. Madame herself was honorary president, and the meetings were held every second Friday afternoon in her own parlor. A chance to gain a place in this pleasant circle was offered to the pupils of the higher classes twice during the year; the aspirant wrote an essay upon a given subject, and if the composition proved up to a certain standard the writer was forthwith received into the club. Wopsie was particularly anxious to become a member, and gladly welcomed the opportunity announced by the *literati* shortly before the commemoration of the Revolutionary Tea Party. Unfortunately, however, notwithstanding her longing to shine, no one was more procrastinating than the Indian princess, unless it were perhaps the indolent Marchésa di Niente.

"Never do to-day what you can put off till to-morrow—that is my motto," Wopsie often declared; her ready memory, and the facility with which she could dash off a composition, had so often served her that she was only too prone to leave much of her work until the last moment. And so it proved in this instance. She had a month in which to write this essay; well, there was no use in beginning early, as several other girls had done. Gracious! she would thus become heartily tired of the theme. And then she had so many class tasks to make up. Mary Renwick and Tessie did not have to write special themes, being already members of the club. And it would not do to let them get ahead of her while she was cudgelling her brains for something brilliant to say about spring—"a stupid subject anyhow."

A fortnight slipped by. Still, there were two weeks left. She would work during the evenings and there was an extra holiday—Washington's Birthday.

Then came the Tea Party frolic, in preparing for which she had forgotten all about the composition, so now there was only one week more.

"Well, I *must* go to work!" she exclaimed on this last Saturday before the meeting of the club, and, accordingly, having finished arranging her room, she sat down by the window, with pencil and an old commonplace-book wherein she was accustomed to scribble the first draft of her exercises.

"Come, gentle spring, ethereal mildness, come," she apostrophized serio-comically, with pencil poised in air. "What can I find to say about it that will be clever enough to suit Miss Langdon and the critical *literati*, since the compositions are to be read before them and the prize of membership is to be decided by their vote? Oh, dear, why did I delay so long? *Spring!*"

She threw down the pencil and leaned back in her chair; her eyes grew dreamy and she stared at the rug on the floor without seeing it. Her thoughts had flown back to a time long ago, almost as long ago as she could remember, when, a little child at the Government agency, she played about the door of her father's plain frame house, the wonder of the reservation. She recalled the joy of their aboriginal neighbors at the coming of spring, when, as they said, the heart of the earth grew more loving with the warmth of sunlit days. The huts and tepees of these poor Indians were indeed, in most cases, devoid of every need of civilization, but at this season all the hardships of the winter were forgotten; for did not the whole bright outdoor world belong to the children of the forest?

Oh, the happiness of those springtime mornings! when the wild birds sang blithely from the trees, the squirrels and rabbits made merry in the woods, the daisies smiled from the pastures where were picketed the clever little mustang ponies; and in the blue sky overhead sailed the fleecy clouds, white-winged ships upon the aerial ocean, bearing away to the Great Manito the petitions of his people. Closing her eyes, she seemed to open them again upon the actual scene, to see reservation after reservation stretching far away. There were crocuses and cowslips in the valleys, and upon the hills beyond wind-flowers, hepaticas, and yellow violets. She saw the creek that wandered through the timberland near her home, and the cliff, far up the side of which, in a narrow fissure, bloomed a little wildwood garden sown, no doubt, by the winds and birds.

And then, in an idle fashion, there floated through her mind faint impressions of the still earlier time of which she had descanted so extravagantly to her schoolmates;—the time when Wankewa, the old squaw nurse, stole after the disaffected Indians of the tribe, taking the little pappoose, the chirping wild-bird nestling of the paleface agent. She recollected dimly how one night during their wanderings Wankewa made her a tiny wickiup in a leafy hollow, where, sheltered from the breeze, she slept wrapped in a warm Indian blanket. After this there was a blank—a confusion of dusky visions, woods, prairies, and streams. The moon waxed and waned, and she was at home again.

And thenceforth her father hardly dared to allow her out of his sight; whenever he went abroad she rode before him upon his rough-coated, fiery little mustang. For several years they continued to live at the agency, but he never knew peace of mind, fearing she might be stolen again; finally he obtained another Government position, and they bade good-by to their strange life at the reservation forever.

Since those experiences the grass had grown many times, but how vividly that life came back to her now! Again, as in a moving picture, she saw the seamed, red-brown, immobile visages of the men who found the tilling of the soil so irksome, and so often made a break for their former roving existence; the patient features of the women, who were still too often compelled to plant and hoe the corn as in the old nomadic days; the preternaturally grave faces of the children, her companions, who yet had their games and plays, which they followed in as weirdly solemn a fashion as though they were taking part in mystic rites.

Ah, if Wopsie had only written about all these things! What better contribution could the Literary Club have asked than these recollections, so different from those of a conventional childhood? But, unfortunately, she did not realize the value of the treasure at her hand; she could discourse upon it in bombastic style, but she did not understand that to write well she had but to try to depict life and nature as closely as possible; this actual Indian life, which she had in a measure shared, would have seemed to her all too rough and mean and rude to have been taken seriously as the subject of an *essay*, even had the idea been suggested to her. And so Wopsie turned from her reverie, unconscious that she was casting aside gems of thought as unique and curious as the string of amber beads about her throat—which still seemed to hold imprisoned in their clear depths something of the golden sunshine and the brightness of those springs of long ago.

But the afternoon was drawing to a close, and she would have so few half-hours to work upon her essay during the coming week. She hesitated a moment, then sprang up, and after bolting the door of the room took from her pocket a key, and unlocked the drawer of the table at which she usually prepared the lessons learned out of school hours.

In the drawer lay a time-yellowed copy of a magazine, bearing a date of ten years before. Wopsie caught it up, turned over the leaves rapidly, and finally stood studying a certain page with critical intentness.

"Why not?" she exclaimed at length. "If this were a school task or a competition, of course I should not even entertain the idea, because it would wrong some one else; but in this case it makes no difference—it is simply a matter of individual success. And who will be the wiser?"

Thereupon, with the book open before her, she began to write rapidly.

* * * *

The day for the formal meeting of the Literary Club came at last. Miss Langdon and the committee passed upon the compositions submitted to them, and it was announced that three of the aspirants had been successful. Wopsie was one of the fortunate trio, but then that went without saying, everybody attested; the girl from the "Wild West" always wrote in such a highly original manner.

Wopsie was jubilant; at last she had gained her enthusiastic wish. She was a member of the club—all that remained to complete the assurance was the welcome to be extended by her friends in the association. That would take place in the afternoon. How she had looked forward to sharing in the delightful

little reunions in Madame's drawing-room!
At the usual hour the club were duly assembled there, while Wopsie in her own room impatiently awaited the summons to join them.

Presently came a knock at her door; she threw it open and in the hall stood Annette, the young colored maid.

"If you please, missy, Madame done tole me to suggest that she wishes to speak to you instanter," said the maid with her habitual mournful air, which was quite out of keeping with the character of a bearer of agreeable tidings; but it gratified Annette to take a tragic view of life.

"Oh, thank you for bringing the message; it is all right," cried Wopsie joyfully, and without stopping to hear more she ran lightly down the stairs.

"Huccome you in sich a hurry?" called Annette, as the impetuous girl started down the second flight of stairs, "Madame done wait on you in the little office yonder."

Wopsie paused surprised, albeit a moment of reflection reassured her. No doubt, the new members were to go down together, and be ceremoniously presented to the club. Accordingly, she turned towards the office on the second floor.

Miss Carstens was, however, the only one with Madame. "Come in, Eva," said the latter, as the girl hesitated upon the threshold;

"I wish to have a few moments' conversation with you."

Miss Langdon always addressed her by her Christian name; otherwise, Wopsie often laughingly questioned if she herself might not have forgotten it. Yet now, strangely enough, it made her vaguely uncomfortable, especially as she felt Miss Carstens' cold gray eyes fixed upon her through those forbidding steel-rimmed spectacles. She flushed slightly, yet managed to return the gaze of the visibly nervous woman with an assumption of dignified composure.

"I suppose you are aware, my dear," continued Madame, "that you have been elected a member of the Literary Club?"

Wopsie inclined her head and quickly recovered her self-possession.

"Your composition, although not in your usual vein, greatly surpassed those of the other aspirants in style and thought," Miss Langdon went on in her clear, well-modulated tone, "but I regret to say Miss Carstens has a criticism to offer upon it."

Wopsie's eyes had brightened with pleasure at the words of commendation, but now again she felt singularly disconcerted.

"What nonsense!" she said to herself; "there is not one chance in a thousand that Miss Carstens—" Then she stopped short in her mental colloquy, and, with a defiant toss of the head, stared boldly at her would-be critic.

Miss Carstens was visibly excited.

"Yes, I am very sorry you happened to hand me the essay to read, Madame," she began, with a deprecating glance at her chief. "It was not in my province—none of my affair at all—"

"No," muttered Wopsie savagely, under her breath, "none of your affair, and I can't see why you should have anything to say about it."

"Nevertheless, since it was, I may say, in a manner forced upon my notice, with words of personal compliment that a member of my class should have so well acquitted herself, et cetera," pursued the little teacher, "and deeply as I deplored the necessity of withholding my meed of approval from the chorus of praise that greets one of my pupils,—a sense of duty—the promptings of conscience, impelled me to express to my principal my true opinion of Miss Thompson's very remarkable essay upon spring."

Wopsie's trepidation increased, but still she anticipated nothing more than a probable difference with Miss Carstens.

"The essay is certainly beautiful," granted that lady, "although I have seen better—that is, less conventional work from Miss Thompson" (here Wopsie's eyes opened wide); "she could have surpassed it, in some points; therefore I deeply regret that she should have stooped to borrow the thoughts of another."

Wopsie's face became a deep, dusky red: "Why, Miss Carstens, what do you mean?" she said fiercely.

"I mean, or rather I strongly suspect—you copied the essay from a printed book."

The girl, whose self-possession had returned at the other's tacit acknowledgment that she had not positive proof for her assertion, now quailed again, but she shut her lips firmly together and haughtily regarded her unexpected accuser.

"My dear, I trust it will prove to be all a mistake; Miss Carstens did right to lay her opinion before me, but I need only your assurance that she is in error, and the essay is your own; for that you followed a train of thought which may also have occurred to some one else is not improbable. There are many instances, too, of the unconscious plagiarism which sometimes comes from reading up on a certain subject," said Miss Langdon earnestly.

Still Wopsie was silent; a struggle was going on within her heart. All she had to do was to say the essay was her own, and Madame would believe her; on the other hand, if she failed to do so, why, there was her membership in the club at stake—her position in the school—

"I should be very glad to have Miss Thompson's assurance that I am wrong," acquiesced Miss Carstens fussily: "I obtained by degrees the impression, which I am, until then, forced to entertain. Upon reading the composition I was first struck by the fact of it being so unlike Miss Thompson's usual style; gradually the sense that I had read passages from it before dawned upon me. I searched in the library, but found nothing like it; then suddenly I remembered. About a fortnight ago Miss Langdon chanced to say there were some old prints in the garret, an overflow from the library. I asked permission to look at them and she gave me the key. While there I happened to pick up a number of a periodical now extinct; in its columns I read the charming bit of description, which is so strangely similar to Miss Thompson's essay. I cannot positively affirm that it is *precisely* the same—because oddly enough when I sought to verify my suspicion and went back to get the magazine I could not find it, and yet—is not this rather an additional proof?"

"I cannot agree with you there, Miss Carstens," interrupted Madame somewhat sharply. "In fact, I am truly sorry the matter has proceeded so far upon such slight grounds. If Eva's composition resembles the extract which caught your eye, I feel confident the similarity is due to a mere coincidence. Moreover the garret is always kept locked and the key remains in my possession. The pupils have no occasion to go up there—the servants are not permitted to do so."

Wopsie smiled grimly. Madame was evidently on her side.

"My child, it is, I dare say, galling to your pride to be called upon to refute this unfortunate imputation, yet I know you would be indignant did I not afford you the opportunity of doing so," pursued Miss Langdon. "Simply your word, my dear, is all I ask."

Simply her word! And yet, alack, that was just what Wopsie could not give. In the flurry and anxiety of preparing her essay, it had not seemed a matter of so much moment to glean a paragraph here and there from the pages of a forgotten magazine, and omit the quotation marks; but now she realized that her attempt to impose upon others by presenting to them as her own these copied extracts was indeed an ignoble act.

It was a critical moment; Madame believed in her, Miss Carstens could be silenced by the answer for which Miss Langdon waited expectantly. Wopsie, however, shrank back affrighted from the pitfall yawning before her feet; true, she might brave it, leap across, and continue on along a very pleasant byway, even though it was not the direct path in which she would walk. But, overwhelmed with remorse for what she had done, she suddenly and stoically resolved to accept the consequences of her fault, in a spirit of atonement akin, perhaps, to that which occasionally called forth the admiration of the early missionaries for the untutored savage.

"Madame," she said, casting down her eyes, while her cheeks burned, "I am sorry to disappoint you; Miss Carstens, you are mistaken in supposing the essay to have been copied entire; nevertheless if you wish to refresh your memory as to the exact wording of the paragraphs which seemed to you familiar, I shall be happy to oblige you with a glance at the magazine, which I found no doubt just where you left it. Miss Langdon, you have evidently forgotten that you allowed me to go to the garret in search of costumes for the Tea Party; I am sorry to have abused your confidence."

Miss Carstens stood aghast. Half incredulous, although her own theory was but confirmed, she stared blankly at the apparently impassive girl; then, with the terse ejaculation, "Well, I never!" she hastily left the room.

Without another word Wopsie also turned to go, but her rigid figure swayed and she would have fallen but for Miss Langdon's outstretched hand.

"My poor child," said Madame tenderly. "This is a bitter lesson for you, yet I am glad you had the courage to acknowledge your fault. You must do your best to reinstate yourself in Miss Carstens' regard; and, for the rest, we will begin again from this hour. You shall have a fresh lease of my confidence and trust. Go to your room now and lie down, for I know by your flushed cheeks you have a blinding headache; the repose and quiet will do you good." And silently putting her own little rosary into the hot hand of the self-confessed culprit, she sent her away with an encouraging smile.

Half an hour later Annette knocked at Wopsie's door and entered without waiting for permission.

"Is your haid berry bad, missy?" she inquired. "Madame done 'dvised me to tote you up a cup of tea; she said you might not find yo'self composed to come down again this evening."

She meant disposed, but came nearer the mark than she dreamed.

"I don't want any tea, thank you," said Wopsie gratefully, raising her aching head from the pillow. "But Miss Langdon is one of the kindest women in the world."

"Right you are, miss," assented Annette with an emphatic nod, as she set down the tray and stole gently out again so as not to disturb the sufferer.

CHAPTER XII.

THE GROWTH OF THE BRAMBLES.

"He who sows brambles must look well to his shoes." Hapless Wopsie was soon to understand the application of the old Italian proverb; for, although she had resolutely striven to retrace her steps, she found her way a very rough and thorny one, and was to learn, by the briery tangle of unfortunate incidents that seemed to spring up beneath her feet as the result of her foolish subterfuge, that "truth is indeed the most precious harvest of the earth."

Miss Langdon, on her part, was confronted by a most unpleasant dilemma. Of course the copied composition could not be permitted to pass, and yet Madame's kind heart yearned to shield unhappy Wopsie as far as possible, for she well knew how acutely the proud-spirited girl felt the humiliation she had brought upon herself. Accordingly, at the meeting of the Literary Club on that fateful afternoon, when Wopsie lay with her aching head buried in her pillow, the honorary president merely stated that Miss Thompson had withdrawn her application to be enrolled as a member of the circle, and those who knew Madame best perceived that it would be agreeable to her to let the matter drop without further comment.

This was very well for the time being; but it would have been vain to expect a bevy of quick-witted, restless schoolgirls to refrain from discussing so startling an announcement among themselves, later.

"What could have induced Wopsie to do such an extraordinary thing?" marvelled Irene Wier, looking much more ready to wage war in support of the dignity of the club, than to play the rôle of peacemaker, as her name implied.

"I do not believe she intended any discourtesy to us," answered Tessie Marron, "but you know her father is coming East soon, and he has written that he wishes to take her to New York for a few days. I dare say, with this prospect before her, Wopsie has no thoughts for anything else."

But Tessie's kindly theory did not gain ground. The majority of the little coterie persisted in considering themselves slighted; a faint rumor, started no one knew exactly how or where (perhaps it was helped on by a chance word let fall by tactless Miss Carstens), a surmise here, a question there; at all events within a day or two the whole story came out. Then, indeed, was the indignation of the haughty *literati* aroused against luckless Wopsie.

"The very idea of attempting to palm off on the committee a composition not her own!" cried Laura Gaines. "Of course she must on no account be allowed to aspire to membership at any time in the future."

"I shall never speak another word to her; she should be made to realize how disgracefully she has acted," determined Irene.

"I'll guarantee she realizes it keenly enough, in spite of the half defiant air with which she keeps away from us," interjected Mary Renwick. "She seems so unlike herself; so listless and indifferent about her lessons, too; I can't help being sorry for her."

This was generous of Mary, since Wopsie's loss of interest meant for her the dropping out of the lists of a pressing competitor.

"Miss Langdon thinks we ought not be too hard on Wopsie," added Tessie, "for she had very little training until she came here, and her acknowledgment of her makeshift was really heroic; she could easily have evaded the avowal."

"I cannot see anything very grand in refraining from a falsehood," said Laura bluntly.

"No, and yet Madame says she could quote instances where the simple telling of the truth has required more courage than would be necessary for the storming of a citadel."

"Oh, well, it is useless to argue the point; at least *I* shall never associate with Wopsie again," and Laura stalked away with her head in the air.

She had, however, but given expression to the sentiment of the school; for although the subject was not dwelt upon openly, the history of the unlucky essay became generally known and Wopsie was shunned by her companions. Among them no one was ostensibly more shocked by the revelation than her whilom friend, Olivia.

"So deeshonorable!" the latter animadverted many times. "And to think I took her for my confidant. How she 'ave deceive me, too! I believe not she is the granddaughter of a great chief. What a country; even your princesses are not real! I shall recognize her no more."

"Livvy has not recovered from her chagrin over the Washington Birthday affair, and no doubt this adds a double edge to the keenness of her sense of honor," laughed Tessie, when the remarks of the young foreigner reached her ears.

Tessie always felt sorry for people who were "down," so to speak, even though it were through their own fault. She thought Wopsie's cup of rue must be bitter enough, and she was not going to approve the inexorable pouring of gall and wormwood into it.

"Olivia is certainly not likely to forget the

joke played upon her, but nevertheless, she would naturally be exceedingly sensitive upon any point of honor; the nobility always are," returned Irene Wier. " I presume it is merely because you want to be contrary, Tessie, that you stand up for Wopsie, but why on this account are you unjust to some one else ? "

"I do not mean to be unjust," responded Tessie, and the fear that she might indeed have been so deterred her from saying more.

The girls who had been concerned in the frolic on Washington's Birthday assuredly liked Olivia less because she cherished ill-will against them for what they had intended merely as a harmless jest. But for the most part her schoolmates considered her sensitiveness in the matter of Wopsie's deception in regard to the essay, a very fine thing and, upon the strength of it, la Signorina became almost popular. The disdain she displayed towards her former friend was much more to their taste than the gentle charity counselled by Miss Langdon. Why, if they did not show their disapproval strongly, who would know they, too, possessed the delicate, fastidious shrinking from everything ignoble and mean, which so distinguished the Marchésa ? Who would understand that their ideal of truth and honesty was quite as high as hers ? Accordingly the outlook for Wopsie's peace of mind during the remainder of the term was by no means promising. But even the incident of the unlucky essay was relegated to the background after a while, by other happenings of school-life.

One of the especial accomplishments taught at Miss Langdon's was fine sewing. Of so much importance did Madame consider this branch of a girl's education, that she instructed the classes herself, giving her pupils the benefit of the exquisite skill with the needle she had acquired in the old French convent of which she so often spoke. Tessie had a genuine talent for beautiful needlework and, having finished a sampler which exhibited proficiency in all the plain stitches, she planned something more ambitious—nothing less than a lace handkerchief for a birthday gift for her mother.

When consulted, Miss Langdon warmly agreed to initiate her into the mysteries of the lace-making, saying: "The work will be tedious, my dear, but your dear mamma will prize it the more because of the exercise of patience it will cost you."

So the handkerchief was begun, and Tessie often carried her cobwebby work home with her and wrought at it in secret on Saturdays and at odd times during the week. In the evening there were always lessons to be studied, but sometimes of a morning she rose earlier and thus gained a half-hour for the fairy-like stitching; in fact, whenever there was an odd moment to spare and she was unobserved, out came the bit of lace work from her pocket and into it was stitched the precious fragment of time.

All the girls at school were interested in the progress of that handkerchief towards completion.

"Show us how you are getting on, Tessie!"

"Is it not perfectly lovely?"

"I don't see how you manage to do it so beautifully!"

"How pleased your mother will be with it, especially since you are making it all by yourself!"

Such were the frequent comments by which they evinced their admiration. Only Olivia regarded it with indifference.

"I care not for zese made 'ome laces," she said, with a shrug of the shoulders, upon one occasion when she chanced to see Tessie at work in the recess of one of the study-room windows. "If I want a 'andkerchief of lace, I shoes zat of Venice or ze lace of Genoa; zese of America I zink looks sheep."

"Of course, there are many kinds of laces," indignantly interposed Laura, who appeared just in time to catch the last words of this ill-bred speech. "I dare say Tessie could learn to make the costly *point* as well as the girls of Genoa or Venice, if she wished to spend her life at it, and wear out her eyes in the bargain. But there is nothing cheap about this handkerchief; Madame says Tessie could get at least twenty-five dollars for it if she chose to sell it. And a handkerchief worth twenty-five dollars is handsome enough for anybody."

"Zat ees ze way you Americana value all tings; according how much zey cost, how much zey will bring!" sneered the Marchésa with a mocking laugh, as she turned away.

"I did not ask her approval of my work," said Tessie, in a vexed tone.

"No, Miss Insolence," inveighed Laura. "How I wish the nabob would hurry up the wedding; for surely, after the ceremony I suppose they will take la Signorina away."

"Oh, have not you heard? The marriage is to be on the fifteenth of June, and immediately afterward the party, including Olivia, are to sail for Europe."

"The fifteenth—and this is the last day of May! Well, that *is* news, Tessie. So we have only a fortnight more to enjoy the society of la Marchésa! What *shall* we do when she withdraws the light of her countenance from us? Well, we must only bask in the sunshine of her presence while we may!"

"Laura, Laura, you are *so* sarcastic!" chided Tessie, yet she could not help laughing.

"Miss Langdon says sarcasm is a two-edged sword, and one is as apt to harm one's self with it as to punish others," returned her friend. "But I cannot refrain from retorting upon Olivia. She *does* exasperate me!"

In a few days more the beautiful handkerchief was finished.

With a sigh of satisfaction Tessie detached it from the pattern, and exhibited it to her particular friends. But all the other girls wanted to see it, too, and quite a little group crowded around her in the study-room with congratulations and many encomiums upon her exquisite handiwork.

"It is fit for a queen," declared Wopsie, towards whom her classmates were beginning to unbend a little. And "fit for a queen" everybody agreed it was indeed; that is, everybody but Olivia, who held aloof, apparently engrossed in trying on a pair of new gloves, which she expected to wear when travelling.

As the end of the term was so nearly arrived, school discipline had been somewhat relaxed, but, coming into the room just then, Miss Langdon exclaimed: "What, girls, taking your recreation in the house this lovely morning? Away to the garden; Miss Carstens is waiting for you there!"

"Will Madame please 'old me excuse, I was going to my room. I 'ave so great much packing to do," demurred Olivia.

"Yes, as you are to leave so soon, I shall not require you to keep up with the school routine," assented Madame.

"I shall be glad to go out," owned Tessie

to one of her companions. "I have spent so many recreations indoors stitching at this handkerchief that I really began to get nervous over it. I would not want to make another soon again. I am so happy that it is finished, and a full week before mamma's birthday, too. Now all it needs is to be carefully pressed with a smoothing-iron." As she spoke she opened her desk, laid the handkerchief carefully on a pile of books, and hurried away to the garden with the other girls.

"Is not the air breezy and cool? Let us have a game of some kind," suggested Emily Carrington.

"We might play prisoner's base," chimed in Laura.

"There is hardly time; just at the most exciting moment the bell for arithmetic class would be sure to ring."

"The new game of pass ball is interesting," ventured Tessie.

"The very thing," cried Irene. "Wopsie, I thought you had a ball?"

"So I have—a splendid one. I will run up to my room and get it."

She started off, and for five minutes or more they waited patiently.

"Gracious, why doesn't she come?" grumbled Laura at last.

Another five minutes passed, and then she appeared short of breath. "I could not find it at first," she said, panting, and tossing the ball to Tessie. They began to play straightway, keeping up the merry romp until summoned by the relentless bell. As they were late going in, Tessie hastily got her slate and book and rushed off to class. When the lesson was over she returned to the study-hall and opened her desk. After one glance into it her heart began to beat quickly in nervous dismay— the lace handkerchief was not where she had left it.

"Nonsense! how fussy I have become over it," thought she. "I must have pushed it out of the way in taking out my slate."

She searched through the desk. No, the handkerchief was certainly gone.

"Oh, well, Miss Langdon must have taken it in order to press it," she concluded, trying to reassure herself. "I must not allow myself to become excited. I won't say a word upon the subject to any one until I ask Madame. It would be rather awkward to raise a commotion, and then find that the handkerchief was all right after all. The girls would think I was so foolishly conceited about my work, too. But, oh, dear, I hope it is safe; I have taken so much trouble, and grown so tired over it."

CHAPTER XIII.

THE QUEEN'S LACE HANDKERCHIEF.

As soon as the lessons of the day were over, Tessie went at once to Miss Langdon's little office.

"No, my dear, I did not take the handkerchief," said Madame in reply to her anxious question. "But surely it is only mislaid! Perhaps you took it out of the desk again, yourself. Or in rummaging about you may have pushed it between the covers of a book, or overlooked it after all. What else could have become of it?"

"I know I did not take it out again, and I have hunted through the desk thoroughly, and opened every book," maintained Tessie, perplexed.

"Then one of the girls must have hidden it to tease you."

"I thought of that;" Tessie's face brightened at the supposition.

"It is, however, a silly and unkind jest," continued Miss Langdon, a trifle annoyed, yet confident that she had divined aright. "Perhaps to-morrow you will find the handkerchief restored to the place where you left it."

Tessie went home somewhat reassured, but her dreams that night were troubled.

In the morning she was early at school. Anxiety had conquered self-consciousness and she eagerly asked of her friends in turn:

"*Have* you seen my lace handkerchief?"

"Why, no!"

"Honest and true, I have not."

"What! You don't mean to say you have lost that lovely handkerchief!"

"When did you have it last?"

Such were the answers she received. Then would follow her flurried story: "I left the handkerchief in my desk when we went out to the garden yesterday, and I have not seen it since."

At the study hour Miss Langdon sent for her and asked if she had any tidings of it.

"No, Madame. Nobody knows anything about the handkerchief."

Madame frowned and compressed her lips; half an hour later she entered the study-room. The girls looked up from their tasks; they understood that a sensation was coming.

"Young ladies," began Miss Langdon, "the very beautiful and valuable lace work upon which Miss Marron has been engaged for many weeks is missing. The only plausible explanation of its mysterious disappearance seems to be the unfortunate tendency of some among you to indulge in practical jokes. The pupil who has had the poor taste to do so in this instance will please bring the handkerchief to me at the morning recreation. I will convey her apologies to the owner. If she has not the frankness and moral courage to do this, however, she may return the piece of needlework to Tessie's desk before noon, and I will not pursue the inquiry further."

Tessie grew alternately hot and cold during this announcement, for of course all eyes were directed towards her. Miss Langdon left the room with an air of displeasure. Her words had aroused a flutter of excitement.

"Silence, if you please, young ladies," the teacher in charge was obliged to demand more than once, and it was with difficulty that the pupils could fix their minds on their lessons. Tessie found it absolutely impossible to study.

During the half-hour of recreation that followed it would have been an easy matter for the culprit to slip away and make the expected explanation to Miss Langdon; but at noon the latter could give Tessie no information, nor had the handkerchief been restored to her desk. Several days passed, yet still there were no tidings of it. Had it really been stolen? Madame would hardly admit the supposition, Tessie herself was loath to believe in a theft, yet whether jester or pilferer, the delinquent had been given ample time and a favorable opportunity to return the missing lace, and nothing had come of Madame's tactful provision.

On the other hand it was indeed almost incredible that there could be a thief among the pupils of Perryville's most aristocratic school. Miss Langdon made one more announcement in the study-room. "Young ladies," she said, "as the handkerchief has not been returned I am forced to the conclusion that it has been dishonestly appropriated. The purloiner,— I do not like to use a harsher word, has still the chance to make quiet restitution. I trust, for the honor and reputation of the school, and above all for her own peace of conscience, she will speedily do so."

Nevertheless, even this appeal met with no response. The week went by; Madame was troubled; what more could she do? The report of the loss spread beyond the walls of her house, for the pupils were naturally excited, talkative, and eager to ferret out the mystery. Their parents were indignant over the whole affair, several criticised Miss Langdon severely, as if she were to blame, and one or two wrote to ask if she dared accuse their daughters, and threatening to withdraw their patronage. Of course these rumors were not long in reaching the ears of Mrs. Marron.

"O mamma," lamented Tessie tearfully,

"to think that you should hear of the lace handkerchief in this way! And it was to have been such a lovely surprise!"

"I am indeed sorry, my love," replied her mother with an affectionate kiss; "and I should have prized very dearly the handiwork over which you wrought so long and patiently. But much as I regret to relinquish any chance of recovering it, you would better beg Miss Langdon not to push the matter farther. I fear all efforts to regain the handkerchief will be fruitless and the discussion will only injure the school."

"I am not altogether willing to yield the point," said Madame, when Tessie preferred her request. "Yet what can I do more in the matter?"

Day after day one or another of the girl's companions would inquire: "Have you heard anything of the handkerchief yet?" And always she answered in the negative or by a shake of the head. Even la Marchésa, engrossed as she was in the prospect of so soon leaving what she termed "zis deetestable country," condescended to express some slight sympathy.

"'Tis strange zis about your lace 'andkerchief," she observed airily. "As eet was only common lace, and not di Venizia, I suppose you do not so much mind. But still, you 'ave gave time to it. 'Tis to me foolish to spend ze time over such gewgaws. With us," shrugging her shoulders, " we zink ze flame not worth ze candle, as you say."

"Mrs. Marron regrets the loss of the handkerchief much more than if it were of *point de Venise*," struck in Laura, who as usual was not far from her friend. "And Tessie does not regard as waste of time any trouble taken for her mother's sake."

"Ho, ho! Not so fast, I 'ave mean no offense, Mees Laura; but you Americana are so *ardente*," flouted Olivia with nonchalance. "Yet 'ave you no suspicion who the purloiner, as Madame say—ah, ah!—who the *purloiner* may be?"

"No, none," was the ready reply.

"Perhaps, zen—I can give to you a littler help."

Tessie glanced at her with quick eagerness.

"Have you an idea? Who do you think—" began Laura impulsively.

"I hardly dare to zink—I just suspec', a ver' littler bit."

"But who?"

"I wish not to say who. Yet you 'ave heard for yourself some one cry, 'Ze 'andkerchief is fit for a queen.' Ah, ah! It will serve for a queen, it seems, ah, ah!" and she laughed scornfully.

"You don't mean Wop—" gasped Laura.

Tessie put her hand over her friend's lips.

Olivia's eyes flashed an answer but she only

said in words: "I don' mean nobody nor nothing, but I zink your lace serve an Indian queen ver' well. Ah, ah—better zan zat *di Venizia*, eh? And if zere ees not a nice sense of honor to rely on, what can be looked for? Eet seems zere ees not so much difference between *stealing* an essay and *purloining* a bit of made 'ome lace, ah, ah!"

"Stop, stop, Olivia," pleaded Tessie, distressed.

"Oh, well, well, as you will," said the Marchésa, fluttering away and leaving the two friends staring after her.

"Do you really think Wopsie took it?" queried Laura.

"No, I don't!" responded Tessie, with decision. "And please do not hint at such a thing to any one."

"Still, it may be so," disputed her companion. "After all, if a person is dishonest in one instance, there is every reason for the argument that he or she may be so in another, and Wopsie certainly showed a great want of principle in the affair of the essay."

"Of course, but has she not suffered enough on account of it? Miss Langdon thinks she has learned the lesson for all the future; she says Wopsie's faults are largely the result of her strange rearing."

"All the more reason to presume she has vague ideas of the difference between *mine* and *thine*," argued Laura. "And then—why, don't you remember?—Wopsie went back to the house for her ball the day your lace was stolen. What could have been easier for her than to slip into the deserted study-room and take the handkerchief out of your desk?"

"Laura! I beg of you!—promise me you will not breathe a syllable of this in the school! I *will not* believe Wopsie had anything to do with the theft, and if such a report got around it would be a great injustice to her."

"Pooh, injustice! not a bit of it!" Laura declared. "But I will be mum on the subject if you wish."

Although she kept her word, and Tessie was the personification of reticence, the conjecture was mooted about after all. No one could recollect just how it originated.

"Why, Olivia, was it not you who told me?" asked Mary Renwick, when questioned as to how she had heard the gossip.

"I? I never say so!" quibbled the Marchésa in indignant surprise. "I know nothing of it—I only hear a young ladee make remark—ze 'andkerchief is fit for a queen—ah, ah! I not understand what zat mean, no more zan you, ah, ah! But my! how droll are you Americana! Such a fracas, a *hullabaloo*, you say, eh?—all about a scrap of made 'ome lace!"

"It was Olivia who told me," reiterated Mary, when la Signorina had passed on.

"Oh, well," allowed Irene. "Naturally she would be particularly shocked. Wopsie's conduct would be particularly abhorrent to her, since she is so punctilious upon all questions of honor. Why, you know she was fonder of Wopsie than of any one else in the school before that unlucky incident of the essay. She told me so once with tears in her eyes, and her voice trembled as she said no one realized what it cost her to break off the companionship. But she acknowledged that she was so sensitive in this respect that she would feel constrained to give up even the dearest friend she had in the world, if that friend were guilty of the least act which could be construed as dishonorable. Such delicacy of feeling was, she supposed, the penalty of having a long line of illustrious ancestors—but she could not help it! I do not wonder this latest development has set her sensibilities on edge, as it were, and she cannot tolerate the recollection that she once gave Wopsie her friendship." Irene and the Marchésa had become inseparable of late.

"But, Renie, you talk as if you were sure Wopsie appropriated Tessie's needlework," objected Laura, whose opinion shifted from one side to the other.

"Indeed, my dear, I am afraid there is no

doubt of it," was the response. " Only do not say I told you."

Thus it was. Everybody in the school was finally convinced that Wopsie had stolen the lace handkerchief. That is, everybody but Tessie, who still refused to believe it; "but then," her companions reasoned, "Tessie was so scrupulous and afraid of judging rashly." And what circumstantial evidence could be stronger? Wopsie had been convicted of a species of dishonesty upon a former occasion. Was it more than a step from this to a material theft? Soon the rumor grew that some one had actually *seen* her take the handkerchief, but this mysterious some one, "being the soul of honor," could not come forward and say so openly.

And then there was Wopsie's conduct when she learned that she was suspected. What a rage she flew into! With what a torrent of reproaches, and scorn, and vindictive Indian epithets did she overwhelm those who had been bold enough to carry the story to her. With what sullen obstinacy she shut herself up in her own room, refusing to come to class, to recreation, to so much as take her meals with the other boarding pupils.

Even Miss Langdon could do nothing with her.

Now how different it would have been if she had *not* taken the handkerchief. Surely, in this case, conscious of her own innocence

she would have laughed at the accusation;
begged Madame to come and look through all
her belongings, and behaved just as usual,
instead of getting so angry and acting like a
young savage generally. Oh, yes, said schoolgirl gossip, even Miss Langdon was satisfied
that Wopsie was the culprit.

CHAPTER XIV.

AN INDIAN SPHINX.

As a matter of fact, Miss Langdon was puzzled and perplexed. She had wished to show Wopsie that she gave no heed to the ugly rumor current in the school, but the girl obdurately avoided her. Wopsie's self-imposed seclusion was of course at variance with all the customs of the house, but Madame thought it best to pass over this infringement of the rules and, after one or two attempts to win her confidence, concluded to await patiently the lifting of the veil of mystery which enshrouded this most singular and inscrutable pupil. So the latter remained shut up in her own room and refused to speak to any one, while down-stairs her schoolmates smiled significantly at the mention of her name, and wondered why she did not ask her father to take her away at once. Tessie alone made repeated efforts to see her, yet every move in this direction proved an utter failure. The recluse appeared deaf to all the messages of this persevering friend; her little notes were returned unopened, her frequent pleadings at the door met with no word of reply. Nevertheless, one afternoon she mounted the stairs, determined upon one more endeavor to force an interview with the voluntary exile. In the hall she came upon Annette.

"I 'clare to gracious, missy," said the maid, "'twould melt the heart of a stone to watch that pore chile; she jes' sits thare like she wuz an image an' don't hardly tech her meals when I brings 'em to her. She sholy is a-pinin', an' I'm opinionated she'll go clar out o' her haid, or be took with a feber, ef she ain't roused somehow. She ain't so flamagatious this last day or so, howsomever; an' I done took notice that she has a little picture o' the Saviour (the one of the Pleading Heart), upon the wall before her; and yisterday she left her room dressed for a walk. I was scared 'most out o' my seben senses when I ran against her comin' down the sta'rs; hit was sort o' like meetin' a speerit from the shadder world. But I rushed for a hat an' made after her, 'case Madame done give me orders that ef Miss Wopsie tried to slip away 'thout lettin' a livin' soul know, I wuz to follow her, eence hit wuz, you may say, powerful unsafe to let her go off alone, an' no one a-sartain but she might do herself some harm, bein' brought up among savages, as I hear tell."

Evidently Annette's notion of Wopsie's former life was as vaguely romantic in its way as the illusion of the Marchésa upon the same subject. Tessie smiled in spite of herself, but the bright-eyed colored girl chatted on:

"Well, not wantin' ter be ongrateful ter my obligations I hurried after her, 'thout lettin' her take no intelligence o' the fact; but Lor' a massy, we wuz way off in our circumlocutions; the pore honey made straight for the church. I slipped into a pew to wait, an' thar, missy, she stayed a considerable time a-prayin' like any pious Christian, an' as ef her soul wuz a-yearning for comfort. Furder mo', ef *she* had to do with the speeritin' away o' yore lace handkerchief I think likely yo're a-gwine to find it onexpected, afore long, an' that's the livin' trufe."

The young girl gave the sharp attendant a searching look, but quickly felt ashamed of the momentary suspicion, for Annette had always been considered "as honest as the sun."

"Miss Thompson knows nothing whatever about my lace handkerchief; I am surprised at you, Annette," she said stiffly.

"For kingdom come I ain't never concerted she did, missy," deprecated the talkative maid. "But it 'pears like she was a-sufferin' the torments o' an oneasy mind, anyhow. An' when I riccollect jes' how merry she wuz in the walks an' ways o' life a while ago, an' I take notice how different hit am now, why, hit done make me so flapdazzled I don' know what to do."

Thereupon, Annette hastily wiped her eyes with her dusting cloth, and picking up the broom she had let fall a few moments before, continued her work of sweeping the hall, while Tessie proceeded up the second flight of stairs. The day was warm and, visitors not being expected, Wopsie's door stood a few inches ajar.

"What a fortunate circumstance," noted Tessie, whose heart beat a little quicker as she approached. When opposite to the room she paused and looked in. Unconscious of her proximity Wopsie sat at the table by the window, motionless as though carven in stone, staring at the small picture on the wall in front of her, with a grave, impenetrable face.

"A veritable Indian sphinx," thought the uninvited caller, shrinking back with a strange reluctance to break the spell of silence. But this timidity must be conquered, she told herself. Now was the time to have an understanding with Wopsie, once and for all. The next moment, rapping lightly, she put her head in at the door, saying:

"Pardon me, Wopsie, I must speak to you." At the sound of her voice Wopsie sprang up as if shot and, facing her with burning cheeks and flashing eyes, cried:

"Tessie Marron, what do you mean by coming here? Please go away immediately. Do you think I have the patience of a saint?"

"No, I do not indeed," returned Tessie,

who also, as evinced on former occasions, had a temper of her own. "But I came—" she added more softly.

"Oh, I know," scoffed Wopsie with a bitter laugh. "You came to inquire about your lace handkerchief, to bother and reproach me, to tease me to give it up, no doubt. I tell you all that will be of no avail, so you may just go away."

She crossed the room and attempted to close the door, but the intruder stood in the way and would not yield. Wopsie glared defiantly. In the eyes that met hers she read a determination equal to her own. She had actually grown thin during this week of self-imprisonment; Tessie noticed this and her heart softened.

"Wopsie dear," she said tremulously, "I came to tell you I do not believe you took the lace handkerchief. I have never believed so for a single minute."

Wopsie faltered, and forthwith, overwhelmed by this unexpected avowal of trust and affection, gave way to a flood of tears, threw her arms around her friend in an impulsive caress, and cried again and again hysterically, "O Tessie, Tessie!" Then, almost as quickly, she pushed Tessie gently but firmly from her, banged the door to, and turned the key, leaving her visitor standing alone in the hall.

In vain Tessie pleaded at the door. "Wopsie dear, let me in! don't be foolish, I want to talk to you!"

Wopsie was obdurate.

"No, no. Thank you, Tessie, oh, so much, but indeed I cannot. Leave me alone, do," she called in a smothered tone through the keyhole.

There was no help for it. Tessie was obliged to give up, and she went home sadly disappointed. Naturally, the next day she confided the result of her visit to Laura.

"Queer, was it not?" she said in conclusion, after describing Wopsie's impetuous embrace and as sudden banishment of her.

"Very queer, certainly," agreed Laura. "Manifestly it can only mean one thing."

"I am afraid it does," acknowledged Tessie mechanically.

"Yes, it proves that she must have taken your piece of work," Laura went on.

"It proves no such nonsense," interrupted Tessie, a little sharply. "Wopsie never stole the handkerchief. I have said so all along, and I am more confident of it than ever, now."

Laura stared at her in genuine astonishment, and finally broke out with:

"Well, I am sure I do not see how you can cling to that conclusion. I consider her manner to you a very suspicious point. If she were innocent would she not have told you so, especially when you assured her of your belief that she had been wrongly accused? But she did nothing of the kind. Her silence is an admission of guilt. Of course, when you expressed such blind faith in her, she felt ashamed and sorry and—hysterical. Perhaps, as Annette thinks, she will return the handkerchief, or may be she has lost it and that makes her unhappy, supposing she would really wish to put it back."

To all these arguments, however, Tessie only shook her head, repeating persistently:

"Wopsie never stole the handkerchief at all."

"Tessie Marron, after her remarkable conduct, why do you keep on saying so perversely that she knows nothing about it!" reproached Laura, exasperated.

"I do not say she knows nothing of it," corrected her friend. "Only that she did not *steal* it."

"Oh, well, I presume you have a charitable way of construing the act. I dare say she *borrowed* the lace work," sarcastically, "but I believe in calling things by their right names, while you speak in riddles. Tessie, I should like to know what you mean."

Tessie sighed. Laura appeared determined to misunderstand her, and, when it came to the point, she did not feel justified in expressing the thought in her mind.

When, hoping to create a more favorable impression in Wopsie's behalf, she went to Miss Langdon with an account of the interview with the suspected girl, she was surprised to find that Madame took the same view of it as Laura. Wopsie's conduct had been very singular, she considered.

"But, Madame," ventured Tessie desperately, "suppose Wopsie knew who took the handkerchief—would not this account for her manner?"

Madame hesitated as if struck by the question, but presently she dismissed the idea with a smile and a shake of the head. "I am afraid in this instance your generosity and wish to judge gently have misled you, my dear," she said. "Unfortunately there is no one else half so likely to have stolen the handkerchief as Eva. Besides, no one else went back to the study-room at the recreation hour during which it was lost. All the other pupils were in the garden."

"Perhaps not *all*, Madame," rejoined Tessie, showing a disposition to argue the point. "Olivia, for example, remained in the house to pack her trunk."

Madame's eyes opened wide; she considered Tessie's persistence carried too far to be consonant with good breeding.

"Olivia spent the time in her own room; I happen to know because it is next to mine," she responded coldly. "Besides, you would hardly accuse a member of the distinguished family of Parmesano di Niente of—"

"No, no—" stammered Tessie, and the expression of perplexity deepened upon her face.

"There is absolutely *no one* to be suspected but Eva, you see," concluded Miss Langdon decisively, and the subject was dropped.

* * * *

"Of myself I can do nothing more to unravel the mystery," declared Tessie to Laura, who, at least, sympathized with her distress over the matter; "but I shall keep on praying to St. Anthony to help me find the lace handkerchief and thus clear Wopsie."

"The dear saint may find your piece of needlework for you, but I suspect even he cannot assist Wopsie so far," replied her friend, who quickly repented the speech, however, when she perceived that it caused Tessie's eyes to fill with tears.

A week passed, bringing the day of the examinations. Even Tessie forgot the lace handkerchief for a time. All the pupils were excited over the great ordeal of the school year. Wopsie alone remained in her room; Miss Langdon, displeased at what she considered the girl's incorrigible obstinacy, concluded that it was better to let her severely alone. The only incident to divert the attention of the girls from their books was the departure of Olivia. Wopsie heard the voice of the Marchésa in the hall. Her face brightened for an instant, and she breathed quicker at the thought that her old friend was coming to bid her good-by. But she need not have felt so strangely constrained and embarrassed, nor have resolved so unwaveringly not to open the door, even for a farewell word.

La Signorina was only haughtily ordering Annette to carry down her satchel, and explaining that her trunk would have to be sent on to New York by a later train, since the expressman had not called for it in time. Wopsie, seated at the writing-table by the window as usual, bit her lips until they were as red as cherries and smiled bitterly at her mistake, as Olivia passed the door, apparently without a thought of her, and ran lightly down the stairs. In the hall below a little group of schoolmates, willing to let bygones be bygones, had gathered to take leave of the young Italian.

"*Addio*, my friends," cried Olivia gushingly, saluting each with a little peck first on one cheek and then on the other by way of a parting kiss. "I cannot in verity say I am grieve to depart from zis so unique school, forever. You know how 'ard eet 'ave been for one like me— But I forgive to all whatsoever 'ave been done against me. We can laugh at eet now—ees eet not so? And the nex' time you 'ave among you some one from a noble family, you will know how to behave better, eh? *Addio*, Signorinas Emiliwahwah and Lauraqua. *Addio*, Mees Tessie Marron; I 'ope you find your 'andkerchief, for, although not di Venizia, eet was not so bad of eets kind; no, not so bad for made 'ome lace." And with this, the nearest approach to a compliment she had ever deigned to bestow upon any one at Miss Langdon's after her break with Wopsie, la Marchésa di Niente disappeared into the parlor where the nabob, now her stepfather, was waiting to conduct her back to the arms of her mother, who professed to be pining for the reunion.

"Insolent to the last!" exclaimed Emily hotly. "I wish we had not stayed to see her off."

"What a pity the carriage has not a place for her trunk," said Laura, peering through the window.

The travellers came out into the hall; they were saying good-by to Miss Langdon. The next moment they descended the front steps, entered the carriage, and presently were gone. Tessie went back to her lessons with a very serious face. An hour later, as the girls were going to French class, they caught sight of the expressman bringing down Olivia's trunk, and banging it against every step of the stairs.

"The last of Livvy," whispered Laura to Tessie, who nodded assent and went on conning a verb. It was not quite the last of la Marchésa though, after all.

The next morning as the two friends came into school they encountered Annette, who upon beholding them threw up her hands, ejaculating:

"O Miss Tessie, chile! O Miss Laura! The queerest thing that eber was, hab come to pass! The idjiot 'xpressman—yet I 'low ez p'r'aps I done got no right to 'spaciate mo' on that subject, considerin' what am come about by reason ob it;—howsumeber that ain't got nothin' ter do with the circumferences o' the case—"

"For goodness' sake, Annette, what are you aiming at?" asked Laura, laughing.

"Well, missy," began the loquacious servant once more, as if striving to collect her scattered wits. "That rampagious 'xpressman—though p'r'aps I ought not ter—"

"Oh, go on; we are willing to regard him as a rascal or not, just as you choose, only do tell us what has occurred," Laura interrupted impatiently.

"Well, then, the idjiot, on coming to the station yisterday afternoon, what did he do but set Miss 'Livia's trunk down on the very aidge o' the platform an' drov' off, 'thout as much as a look over his shoulder at hit. Pretty soon thar' cum a wild enjine tearin' ober the track. An' the next thing, honey, shure 's you lib an' breathe, ef that fool enjine didn't pick up the trunk with a corner o' the cowcatcher, an' onb it along, cl'ar the length o' the depot, as neat as you please, an' prisently toss hit off crushed like an eggshell an' only held together by the straps. The baggagemaster was in a rage, they do tell—but ascertaining o' the fact that the trunk cum from this extinguished 'stablishment he hailed that coon, Pete the teamster, who transpired to be a-passin', an' Pete landed Miss 'Livia's things back to us in a dump cart."

"The Marchésa's wardrobe in a dump cart!" repeated Laura. The picture conjured up by the maid was too much for her gravity, notwithstanding that she was good-naturedly sorry for the ill-luck of la Signorina.

"But that am not all," proceeded Annette, turning to Tessie, who had listened in incredulous dismay. "That am not all; I might go on ter excommunicate furder, but Madame done tole me to say nothin', 'xcept as how she wants ter see you, Miss Tessie, berry particular, in the office, an' I was to inform you ob her wishes the moment my eyes should light on you this blessed mornin'."

What could this mean?

CHAPTER XV.

MISS LANGDON EXPLAINS THE MYSTERY.

TESSIE found Miss Langdon awaiting her in the little office whose window, unencumbered by draperies, was shaded by the overhanging branches of a maple-tree wherein, if one watched long enough, one might discover a robin's nest, and learn many things in regard to the charms of bird-housekeeping. The tranquillity of the garden below reigned in the cool and quiet room, redolent with the fragrance of a cluster of glowing June roses that stood in a simple vase upon the desk at which so much business was transacted.

"Be seated, my dear," said Madame, looking up from her writing as the young girl entered, and motioning to a wicker chair commanding the pleasantest view of the maple. "I have sent for you because I desire you to tell me again the story of the loss of your handkerchief, together with every incident you remember which may possibly have any connection with the unfortunate affair."

Tessie complied, going over the matter in

brief, for it had become very unpleasant to her and she did not like to allow her thoughts to dwell upon it.

"And you have no suspicion, no theory as to the individual who took the piece of lace work from your desk?" asked her interrogator with a penetrating glance, when she had finished.

Tessie hesitated.

"I had at one time," she acknowledged at last, with some unwillingness. "But I gave it up, for it was too absurd to be entertained seriously. Then, too, mother cautioned me that suspicion once aroused is with difficulty allayed, and I suspected first one person and then another until I decided to endeavor to banish it from my mind altogether, as the only way to avoid doing some one injustice. I would rather not talk about it any more, if you please."

"So would I," returned Madame, sighing. "And I promise never to mention the subject to you after this morning. Circumstances have arisen, however, which render necessary the present reference to it. Do I understand aright, that despite the circumstantial evidence, and the strong impression against Eva Thompson, you still believe she had nothing to do with the mysterious disappearance of your lace handkerchief?"

"Yes, Madame," affirmed Tessie, with decision. "I have never for a moment doubted

Miss Langdon Explains the Mystery. 171

Wopsie. I am confident she is innocent, but somehow from the first I have felt that she knows the real culprit, but for some reason is not free to give me a clue."

"And I have come to share your opinion," concurred Miss Langdon most unexpectedly.

"Yes," reiterated Tessie, flushing with pleasure. "Wopsie either feels bound in honor not to reveal what she has learned in connection with the lace handkerchief, or else she does not speak because it is either irretrievably lost or destroyed."

Madame smiled.

"At least I can satisfy you upon one point," she said. "The handiwork to which you devoted so much time and patience, Tessie, is neither destroyed nor irretrievably lost. What would you say if I were to tell you that it has, in fact, been found?"

Tessie caught her breath and stared incredulously:

"O Madame!" she stammered at length.

Miss Langdon nodded.

"Furthermore, it is now actually in my possession," added the good lady, and without more ado she opened her desk and took from it a small package done up in tissue paper, which she placed in Tessie's hands. Trembling with excitement the girl unfolded the packet, and presently gave a little cry of delight for there, looking more beautiful than ever against the soft violet background of the paper, lay *her lace handkerchief!*

Yes, of a certainty, the lace handkerchief over which she had wrought so many hours, for in one corner, exquisitely and intricately interwoven with the graceful scroll of the pattern were her mother's initials, as Miss Langdon had designed, and taught her how to work them.

For a moment or two Tessie gazed at it in speechless astonishment, hardly daring to credit the testimony of her own eyes.

"My dear, I am indeed happy to be able to restore it to you," said Madame, understanding her emotion.

"But how—where?—" she faltered at last.

"In what manner was it recovered you would ask?" pursued Madame amiably. "Well, 'twas assuredly by a most unique and remarkable circumstance. You heard from Annette of the trunk crushed like an eggshell at the railway station, through the carelessness of an expressman. The contents were brought back here in hopeless confusion. I at once sent for another trunk and proceeded to pack anew the wardrobe of the Marchésa di Niente since, as she is to sail for Europe on Saturday, it was important that her luggage should be forwarded to the steamer without delay. To avoid the possibility of any misunderstanding afterward, I thought it well to make an inventory of everything returned in the trunk. 'Twas thus I chanced to open this package; I was reluctant to do so, but could not otherwise complete the list. I expected, indeed, to find merely a pretty ribbon or some such trifle. Judge of my amazement, then, at the disclosure which greeted me! My dear, the wrecking of that trunk may be called simply a peculiar accident, yet I cannot but consider it a providential circumstance. Had it not occurred poor Eva would have left us under a cloud, while—on her part—she would have been haunted all her life long by the bitter memory of a great injustice done to her."

"Then, Madame, it was *Olivia*—" Tessie began, but stopped short, unwilling to utter the accusing words.

"Yes, Tessie," replied Miss Langdon sadly. "It *was* Olivia who stole your lace handkerchief. You recollect, I presume, the day you reported your visit to Eva's room, and our conversation during the interview? When you remarked that Olivia had remained indoors at the morning recreation during which the handkerchief disappeared, I was indignant at the mere suggestion of any connection between this circumstance and your loss, and was satisfied the young lady had spent the time in her room. I frankly admit my mistake; it proves that we ought not to assert a thing positively unless we have absolute certainty that we cannot be mistaken—"

"But I did not really suspect her; I only hazarded the remark to make a point in favor of Wopsie, and afterwards I felt I had done wrong to hint at such a suspicion," demurred Tessie. "Even now, I do not exactly comprehend. Is not Olivia, then, the great lady she was supposed to be? I thought there was no doubt of her position?"

"She is verily the Marchésa di Niente, and descended from a distinguished family, if that is what you mean," said Madame.

"Yet how is it possible that one of illustrious lineage could—"

"Steal?" interrupted Miss Langdon bluntly: "Ah, my dear, the best heritage from a noble race is, truly, a natural inclination to honorable and generous deeds; but, on the other hand, individual nobility must be built upon a firmer foundation than the virtues of one's ancestors. Simple worth dates back farther than the most ancient titles of rank. I have little pity for Olivia. There seem to be no extenuating circumstances in relation to this miserable theft. She secretly admired the handkerchief, chance threw in her way an opportunity of becoming possessed of the bit of finery, and she yielded to the temptation without a shadow of the excuse that might be pleaded by the hungry pilferer encountered in a throng for instance."

"Still, I am sorry for her," said Tessie gently. "Olivia had so few of the pretty knickknacks that girls love. If her mother had provided her with more ribbons and 'folderols,' as Delia calls them, perhaps this would not have happened."

"Possibly not; nevertheless the test of character is not in having what others possess, but in being able, ungrudgingly and without envy, to contemplate their enjoyment of the blessings we lack ourselves. I have written to Olivia that her duplicity has been fully revealed. Her conduct in diverting suspicion from herself by casting it upon Eva; her hardness in allowing another to suffer in silence the penalty of her fault; the fact that she showed no disposition to return what she had wrongfully appropriated—all these considerations make me feel that she deserves little mercy at our hands.

"Of course, as soon as I made the discovery I went at once to Eva," continued Miss Langdon. "The poor child heard what I had to say in stolid silence. No one, I think, can ever fathom how deeply wounded she has been through the unjust arraignment of her by her companions. Towards me on this occasion she maintained at first, as before, a proud reserve in which I now discerned an element of reproach, although, indeed, I had not meant to suspect her, and it was only her own singular conduct that raised a question in my mind. When I went on to speak in severe terms of Olivia, however, she aroused from her apathy and springing up, exclaimed fervidly: 'I beg of you, Madame—the Marchésa was once my friend; I pardon and wish to hear no more against her.' Poor Eva! Untrained as she is, our young Indian girl has really a very loyal nature."

"Well, if she can forgive la Signorina, and refrains from judging her harshly, I am sure I ought to, especially since I have the lace handkerchief all safe again," cried Tessie. "I know every stitch, the setting of every mesh of it almost by heart. How pleased mother will be to have her birthday present after all. O Madame, I am so happy, I wish every one in the world were happy, too! And now, may I go to Wopsie? I want to show her how glad I am that the cloud which she suffered to gather around her, in order to shield an unworthy friend, has dissolved into sunlit air, as I knew it would; but just think how long she has lived in seclusion, like a hermitess."

"Yes, my dear, go to her," assented Miss Langdon readily: "Towards you Eva's heart turns with a warmth of true affection unembittered by one hard thought, for from the beginning you have harbored no mistrust of her."

CHAPTER XVI.

A CHOICE OF HEROINES.

The young girl hurried away to the little room up-stairs. Her joyous knock was like the tapping of a congratulatory telegraphic message upon the door, which this time flew open promptly, and there, just beyond the threshold, stood the hermitess with sparkling eyes and smiling face.

"O Wopsie!" cried Tessie, springing forward and clasping the hands of her resolute schoolmate who had spent so many days in solitude. A wave of emotion swept over the latter's dark face and kept her silent for a moment.

"I knew the mystery would be cleared up; I was sure you had some particular reason for acting as you did," began Tessie incoherently; "but now tell me all about it, will you not?"

"My dear Tessie," replied Wopsie, finding voice at last. "I do not wish to speak ill of—well, of any one, but an explanation is due you, and this you shall have. To go back to the day when your lace handkerchief disappeared so strangely. On that morning, as

I came in from recreation for my ball, I met the Marchésa in the study-room. She was standing before a desk, which she closed hurriedly and with some confusion when she became aware of my presence. 'Why, Olivia, what are you doing?' I said involuntarily. 'Don't you know it is against the rules for a pupil to so much as raise the lid of another's desk?' 'I did but search for a book of mine; I must it in my trunk pack,' she answered quickly, and with assumed carelessness, but looking at her sharply I saw she was really excited and uneasy.

"'If you have mislaid the book you would better ask Miss Carstens or Madame about it; anything found is usually taken to the office,' I suggested. Without waiting to hear more, however, she made good her escape, but as she turned away I noticed peeping out of her pocket the end of a bit of lace. I thought nothing of this at the time, but that afternoon when Madame announced the loss of your handkerchief, all these details recurred to my memory. Yet I had not positive proof, and I had no right to cast suspicion on any one; least of all upon one who had been my friend. I was very unhappy, and very sorry for you, because I knew how much patience and love you had wrought into the web of the beautiful birthday gift for your mother. I purposely spoke of this to Olivia, but without any apparent effect; then I taxed her with knowing more than any one else about the disappearance of the lace handkerchief. She affected surprise and prepared to canter away full tilt upon her hobby of family honor, et cetera, but I kept to the point, and reminded her that when I came upon her that day in the study-room she was in the very act of searching through a desk.

"At this she grew thoroughly angry.

"'What care I for a bit of made 'ome lace?' she almost shrieked, stamping her foot passionately. 'All I 'ave to say of eet ees what every one say—eet ces gone—lost—eet can nevair be found—you understand—*eet can nevair be found!* And zat ees all zere ees to say. Diavalo! what an ado for a scrap of made 'ome lace! Now if eet were di Venizia zere might some excuse be! but made 'ome! how droll! One zing I would to you recall, nevairzeless, Mees Wopsiewahwah, and mak' to believe Indian preencess. You say you met me in ze study-room—Ah, ah, I also 'ave zere met *you!* You tell you 'ave see me at ze desk;—I reply I tak' my book from ze desk of Mees Irene Weir—she 'ave give me liberty to do so; Madame can of her demand if eet ees not ze truth. I have no cause nor pairmission to search ze desk of Mees Tessie Marron. I know not her lace handkerchief ees zere. I 'ave always laugh at her made 'ome lace, zat 'ave no value at all; ees eet to be presumed zen zat—Ah, ah, I can laugh, ze idea ees so *ridicolo*, but, eet ees, indeed, a great affront. Vaugh! I snap my fingair at ze weeked calumny of Mees Wopsiewahwah. Ze next moment, howevair, I am on fire with rage at her treacherous whispairs against ze poor foreigner for ze sake off her own protection. Yet who is zere zat will believ' such a fairy tale? What! ze honorable Marchésa di Niente to fancy a bit of made 'ome lace, as eef she was a lady's-maid? I will forgiv' ze insult because of ze *scherzo*, ze jest, ze drollerie, as you call eet. Of what use could la Marchésa di Niente mak' of eet? But ze Preencess Wopsiewahwah,—zat ees very different. And when eet comes to a point of verity, will not every one—yes, *every one*—believ' ze word of la Marchésa di Niente rather zan zat of Mees Wopsiewahwah, who 'ave—pardon me—who 'ave lost already ze confeedence off her schoolmates by ze unfortunate affair of ze *borrowed* essay? Ah, ah! No; already more zan one say eet ees Wopsie who 'ave *stole* ze handkerchief. Ze Indian lack ze nice sense of honor. To borrow an essay, or *purloin* a bit of lace—where ees ze difference? Perhaps she ees not so much to blame, knowing no better;—still, my faith, eet ees awkward, ees eet not?'"

During her dramatic recital, Wopsie had, without the least touch of malice, and indeed almost unconsciously, lapsed into a perfect mimicry of la Signorina's manner and accent, as her natural talent for impersonation asserted itself. Having repeated the cruel words of the Marchésa she nearly broke down, however, and turning away abruptly, clutched nervously at the amber beads about her neck as though they strangled her.

"The wretch! When it was she who went about, slyly whispering the accusation, and thus diverting suspicion from herself!" interjected Tessie indignantly.

But Wopsie stayed her by a gesture.

"We will not dwell upon the point," she said, passing it over quickly. "As a matter of fact, I soon found that every one believed me the culprit—"

"No, not *every one*," corrected her friend.

"Well, all but you, Tessie dear. I blamed no one, though; I felt I had brought this upon myself. It was the consequence of my own folly. And now how could I boldly protest my abhorrence of the theft, assert my honesty, declare that I might be trusted with untold wealth, and yet would scrupulously render an account of every penny of it. Ah, my dear friend, I had sown the brambles; I must tread the thorny path no matter how painful it had become.

"Nevertheless, had there appeared a chance of recovering the handkerchief for you, I would have spoken. I would have braved the distrust and skepticism of the girls, the polite incredulity of Miss Langdon; I would have pitted my word against Olivia's and told **what** I knew, even though it were only to be ignominiously vanquished in the end. In this case, at least there would have been the satisfaction of having done what I could. But the Marchésa had said most emphatically 'the handkerchief can never be found.'

"'Then she must, in turn, have lost it,' I reflected. She *could not* restore it ! No doubt she would be glad to do so, but actual restitution was now impossible. Perhaps she had not really meant to keep the lace at all; perhaps she merely took advantage of an opportunity to examine it critically, intending to put it back immediately; or at worst, she may only have wished to copy the design. Maybe my very appearance in the study-room that morning prevented her from replacing it in your desk at once. At any rate, something had happened to the handkerchief; she could not, therefore, return it, and she was, accordingly, well-nigh demented. So I reasoned, and, to my mind, this accounted for her reckless denunciation of me; the fear of the disgrace of being found out caused her to catch at every straw to help her to evade the consequences of the act she could not recall. And being in so excited a state she was scarcely responsible for trying to shift the blame upon another. Thus I decided, after thinking it over before the little picture of the 'Patient Heart' upon the wall there. And then, all at once, the thought came to me: 'The suspicion of my schoolmates against me is in this instance unjust, but why not endure it in a spirit of atonement for my former faults? Olivia cannot right the wrong she has done; what a rumpus it will make if my discovery becomes known; that is, supposing my story is believed after all. What a grief to the Marchésa's mother; how angry her stepfather will be! What punishment will be meted out to her? When there is nothing to be gained, why overwhelm with disgrace one who has assumed so proud a position among us, up to the very last days of her stay here?'"

Tessie broke forth into an expression of admiration at the unselfishness of this decision, but Wopsie only continued as though it was the most natural conclusion in the world:

"As for myself, on the contrary, I had, it seemed, no reputation for honesty to lose. Moreover Olivia had been my friend; that she was false to me was no reason why I should not stand by her. I was, indeed, wounded by her insinuations against me (she always had a grudge against me since the day of the Indian Tea Party), but I forgave her, and determined to take upon myself the penalty of what she had done, and to be silent.

"Yet I could not go among the girls," acknowledged Wopsie with a sigh of relief that the ordeal was over. "I did not feel strong enough in my resolution to endure either their covert sneers or repressed dislike; and I was afraid that if stung to anger by some cutting word, I would blurt out the whole story. Miss Langdon's kindness, her reproachful air when she saw I was keeping something from her, and finally, her evident disappointment in me, were hard indeed to withstand. But it was hardest of all, Tessie dear, to keep *you* away; to be deaf when you came knocking at the door; to discourage you by an assumption of harsh indifference. At first I supposed, like all the others, you believed me guilty and came to accuse me, or else because you hoped to recover the handkerchief quietly. You persevered, and then, knowing your gentleness and goodness, I began to fancy you wished to accord me your forgiveness. But, oh, Tessie, I never imagined the real reason. I never dared to hope you trusted me through it all, and though my conduct must have been incomprehensible to you. On the day when you found my door open, and insisted upon entering this room to assure me of your confidence in my innocence, then truly I could scarcely refrain from telling you everything. I dared not let you say more to me, for had I listened I would have abandoned my resolution. And so, ungrateful, hard-hearted as you must have thought me, I fiercely pushed you out into the hall and turned the key in the door."

Tessie nodded smilingly, at the same time brushing away the tears of sympathy which had started to her eyes at the words of her friend.

"One hope I had," pursued Wopsie. "I often heard Olivia's voice in the hall below. 'She will never go away without coming to see me,' I said to myself. 'I do not expect her to acknowledge, even to me, that she took the lace handkerchief, but surely, by at least coming to say good-by, she will show me that she appreciates my motive in keeping silence.' Many times I was disappointed. But about a quarter of an hour before her departure I actually heard her step approaching my door. My heart gave a bound and I sprang up to welcome her.

"What an idiot I was to expect such a thing! The next moment she had passed on, I dare say without a thought of me. She had come up-stairs to look for Annette, with whom she wished to leave some instructions about her luggage. Watching from my window, after a few minutes I saw her step into the carriage that awaited her, and presently it rolled away. I thought this was the last I should ever hear or see of the Marchésa di Niente, and, as you may imagine, my thoughts were bitter enough. But last night when Annette brought up my supper she told me of the singular accident to Olivia's trunk. She was greatly excited over the fact that the Signorina's wardrobe had been brought back to the house in a dump cart, and I was so ungenerous as to laugh a little hardly over the mishap. The idea never occurred to me that any good might come of it to myself. Judge of my surprise, then, when Miss Langdon honored me with a visit this morning. She had ignored me for a week, and I knew I was under the ban of her displeasure. As soon as she came into the room, however, I saw from the expression of her face and her gracious manner that something had happened. Nevertheless, I think you can scarcely realize my amazement when she told me all; when, opening the package she held in her hand, she showed me your lace handkerchief, safe and uninjured, and, to my astonished eyes, more beautifuld than ever. Ah, Tessie, the strange train of circumstances indeed proved to me that although one may bring upon one's self a tragic punishment for what seems at first but a slight fault by comparison; yet, on the other hand, God will right all injustice in the end. I forgive Olivia even though she deceived me to the close, and obtained my silence by a lie. She was my friend; I would still shield her if I could! But, Tessie, truest and best, can you comprehend how happy I am to be fully exonerated? Once more I can breathe without a smothered feeling: once more I can meet the eyes of all the world unflinchingly. All these days I have been like an untamed bird, beating against the bars of its cage and pining to be free—"

"Brave, generous Wopsie!" exclaimed Tessie, kissing her affectionately.

"And yet, I shrink from meeting people again," continued the young Indian girl, faltering now that the real ordeal was over.

But, as it chanced, she did not meet her schoolmates until long afterwards, for that very morning her father arrived in Perryville and took her away to New York with him. Miss Langdon experienced much satisfaction, however, in announcing to her pupils the complete vindication of Wopsie, although, in truth, she touched more reservedly upon the part played by the audacious Marchésa di Niente than the overbearing Signorina merited. But the charlatan Indian princess, with a natural nobility of character in striking contrast to the unprincipled selfishness of the unworthy representative of a patrician European civilization, had made this leniency a parting request.

As for Tessie, the dear girl was as happy as she deserved to be, for she had the great pleasure of presenting the beautiful lace handkerchief to her mother as a birthday gift, after all. And, a few days later, Mrs. Marron gave a charming little lawn party for Tessie and her classmates, which was a grand success from beginning to end.

The boys, Joe and Ben, hovered about the scene, but they repaid their sister's forbearance in overlooking their teasing prank at the memorable luncheon by behaving like models of decorum upon this occasion, and did not so much as tweak the tail of Ermine who, snow-white once more, frisked about on the grass and chased butterflies, as carefree as though she had never in her life masqueraded as a blackamoor, or been worried half to death by a brace of mischievous lads.

May and Toosie, who might have been mistaken for two fairy flower-maidens in their dainty rose-pink frocks, helped Delia to pass the cakes and ices; while Mr. and Mrs. Marron gathered bonbons and tropical fruits from the magically productive branches of the cherry-trees, for the amusement and delectation of the schoolgirl guests.

Miss Langdon was present, and Miss Carstens, too, for Tessie had made up her mind that all old grudges must be forgotten. From New York, moreover, had come Aunt Emily and grandfather, and now upon the pleasant air floated the music of the latter's flute, to which several of the girls danced merrily.

"*Ma chérie*, this is a veritable *fête champêtre*," said Laura Gaines, ecstatically congratulating the young hostess.

"Why compare it with anything foreign?" protested Irene Wier, whose impressions in this regard had changed of late. "What could be more charming than a delightful afternoon in an American home garden?"

"A happy home garden where flourish

thoughtfulness, love, and the kindliest hospitality," added Mary Renwick.

"Bravo, Mary! I heartily indorse the sentiment," cried Emily Carrington, applauding.

"Really, Tessie, I have not had such a good time since the aboriginal Tea Party. Have you heard from Wopsiewahwah?"

"Poor Wopsie," answered Tessie gently. "Yes, I had a letter from her this morning; she is going West with her father, but hopes to come back to school next year."

As though by a tacit understanding no one mentioned the name of la Signorina. The only allusion to the drama enacted at Miss Langdon's during the preceding weeks, was made by the irrepressible Emily.

"Well," she said bluntly, turning from one to another of the little group of friends: "You may take your choice of heroines, but when all is said and done, our own Tessie is the heroine for me."

"*I?*" stammered Tessie in blank astonishment, yet laughing at what she was pleased to consider the absurdity of the idea. "Why, I am only a prosaic, every-day girl!"

"That may be," replied Emily teasingly, yet maintaining her point. "But—I put it to a vote—is it not the girl with an every-day stock of cheerfulness, unselfishness, and patience, who is the dearest, sweetest, and best girl, after all?"

PRINTED BY BENZIGER BROTHERS, NEW YORK.

BOOKS OF DOCTRINE, INSTRUCTION, DEVOTION, MEDITATION, BIOGRAPHY, NOVELS, JUVENILES, ETC.

PUBLISHED BY
BENZIGER BROTHERS

NEW YORK	CINCINNATI	CHICAGO
36-38 Barclay St.	429 Main St.	205-207 W. Washington St.

Books not marked *net* will be sent postpaid on receipt of the advertised price. Where books are marked *net* ten per cent. must be added for postage. Thus a book advertised at *net* $1.00 will be sent postpaid on receipt of $1.10.

I. INSTRUCTION, DOCTRINE, APOLOGETICS, CONTROVERSY, EDUCATIONAL

AMERICAN PRIEST, THE. Schmidt. *net*, $1.50.
ANECDOTES AND EXAMPLES ILLUSTRATING THE CATHOLIC CATECHISM. Spirago. *net*, $2.75.
ART OF PROFITING BY OUR FAULTS. Tissot. *net*, $0.75.
BOY GUIDANCE. Kilian, O.M. Cap. *net*, $2.00.
CATECHISM EXPLAINED, THE. Spirago-Clarke. *net*, $3.75.
CATECHISM OF THE VOWS FOR THE USE OF RELIGIOUS. Cotel, S.J. *net*, $0.75.
CATECHIST AND THE CATECHUMEN, THE. Weigand. *net*, $1.50.
CATHOLIC AMERICAN, THE. Schmidt. *net*, $0.85.
CATHOLIC BELIEF. Faà di Bruno. Paper, $0.25; cloth, *net*, $0.85.
CATHOLIC CEREMONIES AND EXPLANATION OF THE ECCLESIASTICAL YEAR. Durand. Paper, $0.25; cloth, *net*, $0.85.
CATHOLIC CUSTOMS AND SYMBOLS. Henry, Litt.D. *net*, $1.90.
CATHOLIC NURSERY RHYMES. Sister Mary Gertrude. Retail, $0.25.
CATHOLIC'S READY ANSWER, THE. Hill, S.J. *net*, $2.00.
CATHOLIC TEACHER'S COMPANION, THE. Kirsch, O.M. Cap. Imitation leather, *net*, $2.75; real leather, $3.75.

CATHOLIC TEACHING FOR YOUNG AND OLD. Wray. Paper, $0.25; cloth, *net*, $0.85.
CEREMONIAL FOR ALTAR BOYS. Britt, O.S.B. *net*, $0.60
CHILD PREPARED FOR FIRST COMMUNION. Zulueta. Paper, *$0.08.
CHRISTIAN APOLOGETICS. Devivier-Messmer. *net*, $3.50.
CHURCH AND THE PROBLEMS OF TODAY, THE. Schmidt. *net*, $0.85.
CORRECT THING FOR CATHOLICS. Bugg. *net*, $1.25.
DIVINE GRACE. Wirth. *net*, $0.40.
EXPLANATION OF THE BALTIMORE CATECHISM. Kinkead. *net*, $1.25.
EXPLANATION OF THE APOSTLES' CREED. Rolfus. *net*, $0.85.
EXPLANATION OF THE COMMANDMENTS. Rolfus. *net*, $0.85.
EXPLANATION OF GOSPELS AND OF CATHOLIC WORSHIP. Lambert-Brennan. Paper, $0.25; cloth, *net*, $0.85.
EXPLANATION OF THE MASS. Cochem. *net*, $0.85.
EXPLANATION OF THE HOLY SACRAMENTS. Rolfus. *net*, $0.85.
EXPLANATION OF THE PRAYERS AND CEREMONIES OF THE MASS. Lanslots, O.S.B. *net*, $0.85.
EXTREME UNCTION. Paper $0.08.

FINGER OF GOD, THE. Brown, M.A. net, $1.75.
FOLLOWING OF CHRIST, THE. Plain edition. With reflections. $0.35.
FUNDAMENTALS OF THE RELIGIOUS LIFE. Schleuter, S.J. net, $0.50.
FUTURE LIFE, THE. Sasia, S.J. net, $3.00.
GENERAL CONFESSION MADE EASY. Konings, C.SS.R. Cloth, *$0.25.
GENTLEMAN, A. Egan. net, $0.85.
GIFT OF THE KING. By a Religious. net, $0.60.
GOFFINE'S DEVOUT INSTRUCTIONS ON THE EPISTLES AND GOSPELS FOR THE SUNDAYS AND HOLY-DAYS. net, $1.75.
HANDBOOK OF THE CHRISTIAN RELIGION. Wilmers, S.J. net, $2.50.
HINTS TO PREACHERS. Henry, Litt.D. net, $1.90.
HOME VIRTUES, THE. Doyle, S.J. net, $1.25.
HOME WORLD, THE. Doyle, S.J. Paper, $0.25; cloth, net, $1.25.
HOW TO MAKE THE MISSION. By a Dominican Father. Paper, *$0.12.
IDEALS OF ST. FRANCIS OF ASSISI, THE. Felder, O.M. Cap.-Bittle, O.M. Cap. net, $4.00.
INTRODUCTION TO A DEVOUT LIFE. St. Francis de Sales. net, $1.00.
LADY, A. Bugg. net, $1.25.
LAWS OF THE KING. By a Religious. net, $0.60.
LETTERS ON MARRIAGE. Spalding, S.J. net, $1.25.
LITTLE ALTAR BOY'S MANUAL. $0.50.
LITTLE FLOWER'S LOVE FOR HER PARENTS, THE. Sister M. Eleanore, C.S.C., Ph.D. net, $0.20.
LITTLE FLOWER'S LOVE FOR THE HOLY EUCHARIST, THE. Sister M. Eleanore, C.S.C., Ph.D. net, $0.20.
MANUAL OF SELF-KNOWLEDGE AND CHRISTIAN PERFECTION, A. Henry, C.SS.R.

MANUAL OF THEOLOGY FOR THE LAITY. Geiermann, C.SS.R. Paper, *$0.45; cloth, net, $0.90.
MASS-SERVER'S CARD. Per doz., net, $0.50.
MIND, THE. Pyne, S.J. net, $2.00.
NARROW WAY, THE. Geiermann, C.SS.R. net, $0.52.
OUR FIRST COMMUNION. Rev. William R. Kelly. List, $0.28; to schools, $0.21.
OUR NUNS. Lord, S.J. Regular Edition, $1.75; De Luxe Edition, net, $3.00.
OUT TO WIN. Straight Talks to Boys on the Way to Manhood. Conroy, S.J. net, $1.50.
POETS AND PILGRIMS. Batoy. School Ed., net, $1.50; Decorative Ed., net, $1.90.
QUEEN'S FESTIVALS, THE. By a Religious. net, $0.60.
RELIGION HOUR: BOOK ONE. Hannan, D.D. List, $0.28; net to schools, $0.21.
RELIGIOUS STATE, THE. St. Alphonsus. net, $0.47.
SACRAMENTALS OF THE HOLY CATHOLIC CHURCH. Lambing. Paper, $0.25; cloth, net, $0.85.
SHORT CONFERENCES ON THE SACRED HEART. Brinkmeyer. net, $0.53.
SHORT COURSE IN CATHOLIC DOCTRINE. Paper, *$0.12.
SHORT STORIES ON CHRISTIAN DOCTRINE. net, $0.85.
SIMPLE COURSE OF RELIGION. Weigand. net, price to schools per 100, $4.00.
SIX ONE-ACT PLAYS. Lord, S.J. net, $1.75.
SOCIAL ORGANIZATION IN PARISHES. Garesché, S.J. net, $2.75.
SOCIAL PROBLEMS AND AGENCIES. Spalding, S.J. net, $2.50.
SOCIALISM: ITS THEORETICAL BASIS AND PRACTICAL APPLICATION. Cathrein-Gettleman. net, $2.75.
SODALITY CONFERENCES. Garesché, S.J. net, $2.75. First Series.
SODALITY CONFERENCES. Garesché, S.J. net, $2.75. Second Series.

SPIRITISM FACTS AND FRAUDS. BLACKMORE, S.J. net, $2.98.
SPIRITUAL PEPPER AND SALT. STANG. Paper, *$0.45; cloth, net, $0.90.
STORIES OF THE MIRACLES OF OUR LORD. By a Religious. net, $0.60.
SUNDAY-SCHOOL DIRECTOR'S GUIDE. SLOAN. net, $0.40.
SUNDAY-SCHOOL TEACHER'S GUIDE. SLOAN. net, $0.85.
TALKS TO BOYS. CONROY, S.J. Paper, $0.25.
TALKS TO NURSES. SPALDING, S.J. net, $1.50.
TALKS TO PARENTS. CONROY, S.J. net, $1.50.
TALKS WITH OUR DAUGHTERS, SISTER M. ELEANORE, PH.D. Cloth, net, $1.25, ooze leather, net, $2.00.
TALKS WITH TEACHERS. SISTER M. PAULA. net, $1.50.
TEACHER TELLS A STORY: BOOK ONE. HANNAN, D.D. list $2.00.
TRUE POLITENESS. DEMORE. net, $0.85.
VOCATIONS EXPLAINED. Cut flush, *$0.12.
WAY OF INTERIOR PEACE. LEHEN, S.J. net, $2.25.
WHAT THE CHURCH TEACHES. DRURY. Paper *$0.24; cloth, net, $0.45.
WONDERFUL SACRAMENTS, THE. DOYLE, S.J. net, paper, $0.25; cloth, net, $1.25.
WONDER DAYS, THE. TAGGART. net, $0.35.
WONDER GIFTS, THE. TAGGART. net, $0.35.
WONDER OFFERING, THE. TAGGART. net, $0.55.
WONDER STORY, THE. TAGGART. net, $0.35.

II. DEVOTION, MEDITATION, SPIRITUAL READING, PRAYER-BOOKS

ABANDONMENT; or Absolute Surrender of Self to Divine Providence. CAUSSADE, S.J. net, $0.75.
ADORATION OF THE BLESSED SACRAMENT. TESNIERE. net, $0.85.
BLESSED SACRAMENT BOOK. Prayer-Book by FATHER LASANCE. Im. leather. $2.25.
BREAD OF LIFE, THE. WILLIAM. net, $1.35.
CATHOLIC GIRL'S GUIDE, THE. Prayer-Book by FATHER LASANCE. Seal grain cloth, stiff covers, red edges, $1.35. Im. leather, limp, red edges, $1.50; gold edges, $2.00. Real leather, limp, gold edges, $2.25.
COMMUNION DEVOTIONS FOR RELIGIOUS. SISTERS OF NOTRE DAME. Imitation leather, net, $2.75; leather, $3.75.
DEVOTIONS AND PRAYERS FOR THE SICK ROOM. LASANCE, net, $0.85.
EARLY FRIENDS OF CHRIST, THE. CONROY, S.J. net, $1.75.
EPITOME OF THE PRIESTLY LIFE, AN. ARVISENET-O'SULLIVAN. net, $2.00.
EVER TIMELY THOUGHTS. GARESCHÉ, S.J. net, $0.90.
FAIREST FLOWER OF PARADISE. LEPICIER, O.S.M. net, $1.50.
FIRST SPIRITUAL AID TO THE SICK. MCGRATH. net, $0.30.
FOR FREQUENT COMMUNICANTS. ROCHE, S.J. Paper, *$0.12.
GO TO JOSEPH. LEPICIER, O.S.M. net, $1.50.
HELP FOR THE POOR SOULS. ACKERMANN, $0.45.
HER LITTLE WAY. CLARKE, net, $1.00.
HOLY HOUR, THE. KEILEY. 16mo, *$0.12.
HOLY HOUR OF ADORATION. STANG. net, $0.90.
HOLY SOULS BOOK. Reflections on Purgatory. A Complete Prayer-Book. By Rev. F. X. LASANCE. Imitation leather, round corners, red edges, $1.75; gold edges, $2.25; real leather, gold edges, $3.00.
HOLY VIATICUM OF LIFE AS OF DEATH. DEVON. net, $2.00.

IMITATION OF THE SACRED HEART. ARNOUDT. net, $1.75.
JESUS CHRIST, THE KING OF OUR HEARTS. LEPICIER, O.S.M. net, $1.50.
KEEP THE GATE. WILLIAMS, S.J. net, $1.50.
LET US PRAY. LASANCE. Retail, $0.25.
LIFE'S LESSONS. GARESCHÉ, S.J. net, $0.90.
LITTLE COMMUNICANTS' PRAYER-BOOK. SLOAN. $0.25.
LITTLE FLOWER AND THE BLESSED SACRAMENT, THE. HUSSLEIN, S.J. net, $0.50.
LITTLE MANUAL OF ST. ANTHONY. LASANCE. net, $0.35.
LITTLE MANUAL OF ST. JOSEPH. LINGS. net, $0.25.
LITTLE MANUAL OF ST. RITA. McGRATH. $0.90.
LITTLE MASS BOOK, THE. LYNCH. Paper, *$0.10.
LITTLE OFFICE OF THE BLESSED VIRGIN MARY. In Lat.-Eng. net, $1.50; in Latin only, net, $1.25.
LITTLE OFFICE OF THE IMMACULATE CONCEPTION. Paper. *$0.08.
MANNA OF THE SOUL. Vestpocket Edition. A little Book of Prayer for Men and Women. By Rev. F. X. LASANCE. Oblong, 32mo. $0.85.
MANNA OF THE SOUL. A Book of Prayer for Men and Women. By Rev. F. X. LASANCE. Extra Large Type Edition. 544 pages, 16mo. $1.75.
MANNA OF THE SOUL. Prayer-Book by Rev. F. X. LASANCE. Thin Edition. Im. leather. $1.25.
MANNA OF THE SOUL. Prayer-Book by Rev. F. X. LASANCE. Thin Edition with Epistles and Gospels. $1.50.
MANUAL OF THE HOLY EUCHARIST. LASANCE. Imitation leather, limp, red edges. net, $1.75.
MARY, HELP OF CHRISTIANS. HAMMER, O.F.M. net. $1.60.
MASS DEVOTIONS AND READINGS ON THE MASS. LASANCE. Im. leather, limp, red edges. net, $1.75.

MASS FOR CHILDREN, THE. KELLY. net $0.26; net, $0.21.
MEDITATIONS FOR EVERY DAY IN THE YEAR ON THE LIFE OF OUR LORD. VERCRUYSSE, S.J. 2 vols. net, $4.50.
MEDITATIONS FOR THE USE OF THE SECULAR CLERGY. CHAIGNON, S.J. 2 vols. net, $7.00.
MEDITATIONS ON THE SEVEN WORDS OF OUR LORD ON THE CROSS. PERRAUD. net, $1.00.
MEDITATIONS ON THE LIFE, THE TEACHING AND THE PASSION OF JESUS CHRIST. ILG-CLARKE. 2 vols. net, $5.00.
MEDITATIONS ON THE SUFFERINGS OF JESUS CHRIST. PERINALDO. net, $0.85.
MENDING THE NETS. MORNING-STAR SERIES II. FEELY, S.J. net, $0.60.
MISSION REMEMBRANCE OF THE REDEMPTORIST FATHERS. GEIERMANN, C.SS.R. $0.90.
MOMENTS BEFORE THE TABERNACLE. RUSSELL, S.J. net, $0.60.
MORE SHORT SPIRITUAL READINGS FOR MARY'S CHILDREN. CECILIA. net, $0.95.
MOST BELOVED WOMAN, THE. GARESCHÉ, S.J. net, $0.98.
MY GOD AND MY ALL. A Prayer-Book for Children. By Rev. F. X. LASANCE. Black or white, cloth, square corners, white edges, retail, $0.35. Imit. leather, black or white, seal grain, gold edges, retail, $0.70. Persian Morocco, gold side and edges, retail, $1.25. Same, white leather, retail, $1.50. Celluloid, retail, $1.00; with Indulgence Cross, retail, $1.35.
MY PRAYER-BOOK. Happiness in Goodness. Reflections, Counsels, Prayers, and Devotions. By Rev. F. X. LASANCE. 16mo. Seal grain cloth, stiff covers, $1.35. Imitation leather, limp, marred corners, red edges, $1.50; gold edges, $2.40. Real leather, gold edges, $3.85.

MY PRAYER-BOOK. Extra Large Type Edition. By Rev. F. X. Lasance. Seal grain cloth, stiff covers, square corners, red edges, $1.75. Imitation leather, round corners, red edges, $2.00. Imitation leather, round corners, gold edges, $2.75. American seal, limp, gold side, gold edges, $3.25.

MYSTERY OF LOVE, THE. Lepicier, O.S.M. net, $1.50.

NEW MISSAL FOR EVERY DAY, THE. Complete Missal in English for Every Day in the Year. New 1924 Edition. With Introduction Notes, and a Book of Prayer. By Rev. F. X. Lasance. Oblong, 32mo. Imitation leather. $2.75.

NEW MISSAL FOR EVERY DAY. (Student's Edition.) By Rev. F. X. Lasance. Retail $1.75.

NEW TESTAMENT. 12mo edition. Large type. Cloth, net, $1.75; 32mo edition. Flexible, net, $0.45; cloth, net, $0.80; Amer. seal, net, $1.35.

NEW TESTAMENT AND PRAYER-BOOK COMBINED. net, $0.85.

NOVENA IN HONOR OF SAINT THERESE OF THE CHILD JESUS. Coleman, net, $0.15.

OFFICE OF HOLY WEEK, COMPLETE. Latin and English. Cut flush, net, $0.45; silk cloth, net, $0.60; Am. seal, red edges, net, $1.25.

OUR FAVORITE DEVOTIONS. Lings. net, $1.00.

OUR FAVORITE NOVENAS. Lings. net, $1.00.

OUR LADY BOOK. By Rev. F. X. Lasance. Imitation leather, limp, round corners, red edges, $1.85. Morocco Grain, Imitation Leather, gold edges, $2.50. American Seal, limp, gold side, gold edges, $3.00. Rutland, limp, red under gold edges, $3.75. Turkey Morocco, limp, gold roll, red under gold edges, $4.75.

OUTLINE MEDITATIONS. Cecilia. net, $1.75.

PATHS OF GOODNESS, THE. Garesché, S.J. net, $4.50.

POCKET PRAYER-BOOK. Cloth. net, $0.45.

POLICEMEN'S AND FIREMEN'S COMPANION. McGrath. $0.35.

PRAYER-BOOK FOR RELIGIOUS. Lasance. 16mo. Imitation leather, limp, red edges, net, $2.50.

PRAYERS FOR OUR DEAD. McGrath. Cloth, $0.35; imitation leather, $0.75.

PRISONER OF LOVE. Prayer-Book by Father Lasance. Im. leather, limp, red edges, $2.00.

REFLECTIONS FOR RELIGIOUS. Lasance. net, $2.50.

REJOICE IN THE LORD. Prayer-Book by Father Lasance. $1.75.

ROSARY NOVENAS TO OUR LADY. Lacey. net, $0.15.

ROSARY, THE CROWN OF MARY. Dominican Father. 16mo, paper. *$0.12.

ROSE WREATH FOR THE CROWNING, A. Rev. John F. Clarke. net, $1.00.

RULES OF LIFE FOR THE PASTOR OF SOULS. Sammerauch. net, $0.45.

SACRED HEART BOOK. Prayer-Book by Father Lasance. Im. leather, limp, red edges. $1.75.

SECRET OF SANCTITY. Casset, S.J. net, $0.85.

SERAPHIC GUIDE, THE. $1.00

SHORT MEDITATIONS FOR EVERY DAY. Lasausse. net, $0.85.

SHORT VISITS TO THE BLESSED SACRAMENT. Lasance. net, $0.35.

SOLDIERS' AND SAILORS' COMPANION. McGrath. Vest-pocket shape, silk cloth or khaki. $0.35.

SOUVENIR OF THE NOVITIATE. Taylor. net, $0.85.

SPIRIT OF SACRIFICE, THE, AND THE LIFE OF SACRIFICE IN THE RELIGIOUS STATE. Giraud. net, $3.00.

SPIRITUAL CONFERENCES. Buckler, O.P. net, $0.85.

SUNDAY MISSAL, THE. Lasance. Im. leather, limp, red edges, $1.50.

TEACHINGS OF THE LITTLE FLOWER, THE. Garesché, S.J. net, $1.25.
THINGS IMMORTAL, THE. Garesché, S.J. net, $0.90.
THOUGHTS FOR TODAY. MORNING-STAR SERIES I. Feely, S.J. net, $0.60.
THOUGHTS ON THE RELIGIOUS LIFE. Lasance. Im. leather, limp, red edges, net, $2.50.
THY KINGDOM COME. SERIES I. Moffatt, S.J. net, $0.30.
THY KINGDOM COME. SERIES II. Moffatt, S.J. net, $0.30.
THY KINGDOM COME. SERIES III. Moffatt, S.J. net, $0.30.
THY KINGDOM COME. SERIES IV. Moffatt, S.J. net, $0.30.
TRUE SPOUSE OF CHRIST. Liguori. net, $1.75.
VALUES EVERLASTING, THE. Garesché, S.J. net, $0.90.
VENERATION OF THE BLESSED VIRGIN. Rohner-Brennan. net, $0.85.
VIGIL HOUR, THE. Ryan, S.J. Paper, *$0.12.
VISITS TO JESUS IN THE TABERNACLE. Lasance. Im. leather, limp, red edges, $2.00.
VISITS TO THE MOST HOLY SACRAMENT. Liguori. net, $0.90.
WAY OF THE CROSS. Paper. *$0.08.
WAY OF THE CROSS, THE. Very large-type edition. Method of St. Alphonsus Liguori. *$0.20.
WAY OF THE CROSS. Eucharistic method. *$0.15.
WAY OF THE CROSS. Method of St. Francis of Assisi. *$0.15.
WITH GOD. Prayer-Book by Father Lasance. Im. leather, limp, red edges, $2.00.
YEARNING FOR GOD. Williams, S.J. net, $1.50.
YOUNG MAN'S GUIDE, THE. Prayer-Book by Father Lasance. Seal grain cloth, stiff covers, red edges, $1.35. Im. leather, limp, red edges, $1.50; gold edges, $2.00.
YOUR INTERESTS ETERNAL. Garesché, S.J. net, $0.90.
YOUR NEIGHBOR AND YOU. Garesché, S.J. net, $0.90.
YOUR OWN HEART. Garesché, S.J. net, $0.90.
YOUR SOUL'S SALVATION. Garesché, S.J. net, $0.90.

III. THEOLOGY, LITURGY, HOLY SCRIPTURE, PHILOSOPHY, SCIENCE, CANON LAW

ALTAR PRAYERS. Edition A: English and Latin, net, $1.75. Edition B: German-English-Latin, net, $2.00.
ANNOUNCEMENT BOOK. 12mo. net, $2.50.
AUTOBIOGRAPHY OF AN OLD BREVIARY. Heuser, D.D. net, $1.75.
BAPTISMAL RITUAL. 12mo. net, $1.50.
BENEDICENDA. Schultz. net, $2.75.
BURIAL RITUAL. Cloth, net, $2.50; sheepskin, net, $3.75.
CHRIST'S TEACHING CONCERNING DIVORCE. Gigot. net, $$0.67.
COMBINATION RECORD FOR SMALL PARISHES. net, $8.00.
COMPENDIUM SACRÆ LITURGIÆ. Wapelhorst, O.F.M. net, $3.00.
GENERAL INTRODUCTION TO THE STUDY OF THE HOLY SCRIPTURES. Gigot. net, $4.00.
GENERAL INTRODUCTION TO THE STUDY OF THE HOLY SCRIPTURES. Abridged edition. Gigot. net, $2.75.
HOLY BIBLE, THE. Large type, handy size. Cloth, $2.50.
HYMNS OF THE BREVIARY AND MISSAL, THE. Britt, O.S.B. net, $3.00.
JESUS LIVING IN THE PRIEST. Millet, S.J.-Byrne. net, $3.25.
LIBER STATUS ANIMARUM, or Parish Census Book. Large edition, size, 14x16 inches. 100 Families, 200 pp., half leather, net, $7.00; 200 Families, 400 pp., half leather, net, $8.00; Pocket Edition. net, $0.50.

MARRIAGE LEGISLATION IN THE NEW CODE. AYRINHAC, S.S. *net*, $2.50.
MARRIAGE RITUAL. Cloth, gilt edges, *net*, $2.50; sheepskin, gilt edges, *net*, $3.75.
MISSALE ROMANUM. Benziger Brothers' Authorized Vatican Edition. Black or Red Amer. morocco, gold edges, *net*, $15.00; Red Amer. morocco, gold stamping and edges, *net*, $17.50. Red finest quality morocco, red under gold edges, *net*, $22.00.
MORAL PRINCIPLES AND MEDICAL PRACTICE. COPPENS, S.J.-SPALDING, S.J. *net*, $2.50.
OUTLINES OF JEWISH HISTORY. GIGOT, D.D. *net*, $2.75.
OUTLINES OF NEW TESTAMENT HISTORY. GIGOT. *net*, 1$2.75.
PASTORAL THEOLOGY. STANG. *net*, 1$2.25.
PENAL LEGISLATION IN THE NEW CODE OF CANON LAW. AYRINHAC, S.S. *net*, $3.00.

PEW COLLECTION AND RECEIPT BOOK. Indexed. 11x8 inches, *net*, $3.00.
PREPARATION FOR MARRIAGE. MCHUGH, O.P. *net*, $8.48.
RECORD OF BAPTISMS. 200 pages, 700 entries, *net*, $7.98. 400 pages. 1400 entries, *net*, $10.00. 600 pages, 2100 entries, *net*, $12.00.
RECORD OF CONFIRMATIONS. *net*, $6.00.
RECORD OF FIRST COMMUNIONS. *net*, $6.00.
RECORD OF INTERMENTS *net*, $6.00.
RECORD OF MARRIAGES. Size 14x10 inches. 200 pages, 700 entries, *net*, $7.00. 400 pages, 1400 entries, *net* $10.00.. 600 pages, 2100 entries, *net*, $12.00.
RITUALE COMPENDIOSUM. Cloth, *net*, $1.25; seal, *net*, $2.00.
SPECIAL INTRODUCTION TO THE STUDY OF THE OLD TESTAMENT. GIGOT. Part I, *net*, 1$2.75. Part II, *net*, 1$3.25.
TEXTUAL CONCORDANCE OF THE HOLY SCRIPTURES. WILLIAMS. *net*, $5.75.

IV. SERMONS

EIGHT-MINUTE SERMONS. DEMOUY. 2 vols., *net*, $4.00.
FUNERAL SERMONS. WIRTH, O.S.B. *net*, $3.00.
HINTS TO PREACHERS. HENRY, Litt.D. *net*, $1.90.
POPULAR SERMONS ON THE CATECHISM. BAMBERG-THURSTON, S.J. 3 vols., *net*, $7.50.
SERMONS. CANON SHEEHAN. *net*, $3.00.
SERMONS. WHELAN, O.S.A. *net*, $2.00.

SERMONS FOR THE SUNDAYS AND CHIEF FESTIVALS OF THE ECCLESIASTICAL YEAR. POTTGIESSER, S.J. 2 vols., *net*, $5.00.
SODALITY CONFERENCES. GARESCHÉ, S.J. *net*, $2.75. First Series.
SODALITY CONFERENCES. GARESCHÉ, S.J. *net*, $2.75. Second Series.
THREE-MINUTE HOMILIES. McDONOUGH. *net*, $2.00.

V. HISTORY, BIOGRAPHY, HAGIOLOGY, TRAVEL

CHILD'S LIFE OF ST. JOAN OF ARC. MANNIX. *net*, $1.50.
HISTORY OF THE CATHOLIC CHURCH. BRUECK. 2 vols., *net*, $5.50.
HISTORY OF THE PROTESTANT REFORMATION. CORBETT-GASQUET. *net*, $0.85.
HISTORY OF THE MASS. O'BRIEN. *net*, $2.00.
IDEALS OF ST. FRANCIS OF ASSISI, THE. FELDER, O.M. Cap. *net*, $4.00.

ILLUSTRATED LIVES OF PATRON SAINTS FOR BOYS. MANNIX. *net*, $1.00.
ILLUSTRATED LIVES OF PATRON SAINTS FOR GIRLS MANNIX. *net*, $1.00.
IN THE WORKSHOP OF ST. JOSEPH. HEUSER, D.D. *net*, $2.75.
LIFE OF ST. MARGARET MARY ALACOQUE. Illustrated. BOUGAUD. *net*, $1.84.

LIFE OF CHRIST. Businger-Brennan. Illustrated. Full morocco, gilt edges, net, $15.00.
LIFE OF CHRIST. Illustrated. Businger-Mullett. net, $1.00.
LIFE OF CHRIST. Cochem. net, $1.85.
LIFE OF ST. IGNATIUS LOYOLA. Genelli, S.J. net, $0.56.
LIFE OF MADEMOISELLE LE GRAS. net, $0.85.
LIFE OF THE BLESSED VIRGIN. Rohner. net, $0.85.
LITTLE LIVES OF THE SAINTS FOR CHILDREN. Berthold. net, $0.75.
LITTLE PICTORIAL LIVES OF THE SAINTS. With 460 illustrations. net, $2.00.
LIVES OF THE SAINTS. Butler. Paper, $0.25; cloth, net, $0.85.
LOURDES. Clarke, S.J. net, $0.85.
MARY THE QUEEN. By a Religious. net, $0.60.
MILL TOWN PASTOR, A. Conroy, S.J. net, $1.75.
OUR NUNS. Lord, S.J. Regular Edition, $1.75; DeLuxe Edition, net, $3.00.
OUR OWN ST. RITA. Corcoran. O.S.A. net, $1.50.
PASSIONISTS, THE. Ward, C.P. net, $4.00.
PATRON SAINTS FOR CATHOLIC YOUTH. By M. E. Mannix. Each life separately in attractive colored paper cover with illustration on front cover. Each 10 cents postpaid; per 25 copies, assorted, net, $1.75; per 100 copies, assorted, net, $6.75. Sold only in packages containing 5 copies of one title.
For Boys: St. Joseph; St. Aloysius; St. Anthony; St. Bernard; St. Martin; St. Michael; St. Francis Xavier; St. Patrick; St. Charles; St. Philip.
The above can be had bound in 1 volume, cloth, net, $1.00.
For Girls: St. Ann; St. Agnes; St. Teresa; St. Rose of Lima; St. Cecilia; St. Helena; St. Bridget; St. Catherine; St. Elizabeth; St. Margaret.
The above can be had bound in 1 volume, cloth, net, $1.00.
PICTORIAL LIVES OF THE SAINTS. With nearly 400 illustrations and over 600 pages, net, $5.00.
POPULAR LIFE OF ST. TERESA. L'Abbé Joseph. net, $0.85.
ROMA. Pagan Subterranean and Modern Rome in Word and Picture. By Rev. Albert Kuhn, O.S.B., D.D. Preface by Cardinal Gibbons. 617 pages, 744 illustrations. 46 full-page inserts, 3 plans of Rome in colors. 8½x12 inches. Red im. leather, gold side. net, $12.00.
ROMAN CURIA AS IT NOW EXISTS. Martin, S.J. net, $0.80.
ST. ANTHONY. Ward. net, $0.85.
ST. JOAN OF ARC. Lynch, S.J. Illustrated. net, $2.75.
ST. JOHN BERCHMANS. Delehaye, S.J. - Semple, S.J. net, $1.50.
SHORT LIFE OF CHRIST, A. McDonough. net, $0.15.
SHORT LIVES OF THE SAINTS. Donnelly. net, $0.90.
STORY OF JESUS, THE. Mulhollahd. net, $0.50.
STORY OF THE DIVINE CHILD. Told for Children. Lings. net, $0.60.
STORY OF THE ACTS OF THE APOSTLES. Lynch, S.J. Illustrated. net, $2.75.
STORY OF THE LITTLE FLOWER, THE. Lord, S.J. Retail, $0.15 net to Priests and Religious, $0.10.
WHISPERINGS OF THE CARIBBEAN. Williams, S.J. net, $2.00.
WONDER STORY, THE. Taggart. Illustrated Board covers, net, $0.35; per 100, $31.50. Also an edition in French and Polish at same prices.

VI. JUVENILES

FATHER FINN'S BOOKS. Each, net, $1.00.
SUNSHINE AND FRECKLES.

LORD BOUNTIFUL.
ON THE RUN.
BOMBY IN MOVIELAND.

FACING DANGER.
HIS LUCKIEST YEAR. A Sequel to "Lucky Bob."
LUCKY BOB.
PERCY WYNN; OR, MAKING A BOY OF HIM.
TOM PLAYFAIR; OR, MAKING A START.
CLAUDE LIGHTFOOT; OR, HOW THE PROBLEM WAS SOLVED.
HARRY DEE; OR, WORKING IT OUT.
ETHELRED PRESTON; OR, THE ADVENTURES OF A NEW COMER.
THE BEST FOOT FORWARD; AND OTHER STORIES.
"BUT THY LOVE AND THY GRACE."
CUPID OF CAMPION.
THAT FOOTBALL GAME, AND WHAT CAME OF IT.
THE FAIRY OF THE SNOWS.
THAT OFFICE BOY.
HIS FIRST AND LAST APPEARANCE.
MOSTLY BOYS. SHORT STORIES.
FATHER SPALDING'S BOOKS. Each, net, $1.00.
STRANDED ON LONG BAR.
IN THE WILDS OF THE CANYON.
SIGNALS FROM THE BAY TREE.
HELD IN THE EVERGLADES.
AT THE FOOT OF THE SANDHILLS.
THE CAVE BY THE BEECH FORK.
THE SHERIFF OF THE BEECH FORK.
THE CAMP BY COPPER RIVER.
THE RACE FOR COPPER ISLAND.
THE MARKS OF THE BEAR CLAWS.
THE OLD MILL ON THE WITHROSE.
THE SUGAR CAMP AND AFTER.
ADVENTURE WITH THE APACHES. Ferry. net, $0.60.
ALTHEA. Nirdlinger. net, $0.85.
AS GOLD IN THE FURNACE. Copus, S.J. net, $0.85.

AS TRUE AS GOLD. Mannix. net, $0.60.
AT THE FOOT OF THE SANDHILLS. Spalding, S.J. net, $1.00.
AWAKENING OF EDITH, THE. Illustrated. Specking. net, $1.50.
BERKLEYS, THE. Wight. net, $0.60.
BEST FOOT FORWARD, THE. Finn, S.J. net, $1.00.
BETWEEN FRIENDS. Aumerle. net, $0.85.
BISTOURI. Melandri net, $0.60.
BLISSYLVANIA POST-OFFICE. Taggart. net, $0.60.
BOBBY IN MOVIELAND. Finn, S.J. net, $1.00.
BOB O'LINK. Waggaman. net, $0.60.
BROWNIE AND I. Aumerle. net, $0.85.
BUNT AND BILL. Mulholland. net, $0.60.
"BUT THY LOVE AND THY GRACE." Finn, S.J. net, $1.00.
BY BRANSCOME RIVER. Taggart. net, $0.60.
CAMP BY COPPER RIVER. Spalding, S.J. net, $1.00.
CAPTAIN TED. Waggaman. net, $1.25.
CAVE BY THE BEECH FORK. Spalding, S.J. net, $1.00.
CHILDREN OF CUPA. Mannix. net, $0.60.
CHILDREN OF THE LOG CABIN. Delamare. net, $0.85.
CLARE LORAINE. "Lee." net, $0.85.
CLAUDE LIGHTFOOT. Finn, S.J. net, $1.00.
COBRA ISLAND. Boyton, S.J. net, $1.25.
CUPA REVISITED. Mannix. net, $0.60.
CUPID OF CAMPION. Finn, S.J. net, $1.00.
DADDY DAN. Waggaman. net, $0.60.
DAN'S BEST ENEMY. Holland, S.J. net, $1.25.
DEAR FRIENDS. Nirdlinger. net, $0.85.
DEAREST GIRL, THE. Taggart. net, $1.50.
DIMPLING'S SUCCESS. Mulholland. net, $0.60.
ETHELRED PRESTON. Finn, S.J. net, $1.00.

EVERY-DAY GIRL, AN. Crowley. net, $0.60.
FACING DANGER. Finn, S.J. net, $1.00.
FAIRY OF THE SNOWS. Finn, S.J. net, $1.00.
FINDING OF TONY. Waggaman. net, $1.25.
FIVE BIRDS IN A NEST. Delamare. net, $0.85.
FOR THE WHITE ROSE. Hinkson. net, $0.60.
FRED'S LITTLE DAUGHTER. Smith. net, $0.60.
FREDDY CARR'S ADVENTURES. Garrold, S.J. net, $0.85.
FREDDY CARR AND HIS FRIENDS. Garrold, S.J. net, $0.85.
GOLDEN LILY, THE. Hinkson. net, $0.60.
GREAT CAPTAIN, THE. Hinkson. net, $0.60.
HALDEMAN CHILDREN, THE. Mannix. net, $0.60.
HARMONY FLATS. Whitmire. net, $0.85.
HARRY DEE. Finn, S.J. net, $1.00.
HARRY RUSSELL. Copus, S.J. net, $0.85.
HEIR OF DREAMS, AN. O'Malley. net, $0.60.
HELD IN THE EVERGLADES. Spalding, S.J. net, $1.00.
HIS FIRST AND LAST APPEARANCE. Finn, S.J. net, $1.00.
HIS LUCKIEST YEAR. Finn, S.J. net, $1.00.
HO!-AH! McDonald. net, $1.25
HOSTAGE OF WAR, A. Bonesteel. net, $0.60.
HOW THEY WORKED THEIR WAY. Egan. net, $0.85.
IN QUEST OF ADVENTURE. Mannix. net, $0.60.
IN QUEST OF THE GOLDEN CHEST. Barton. net, $0.85.
IN THE WILDS OF THE CANYON. Spalding, S.J. net, $1.00.
JACK. By a Religious, H. C. J. net, $0.60.
JACK O'LANTERN. Waggaman. net, $0.60.
JACK HILDRETH ON THE NILE. Taggart. net, $0.85.
JUNIORS OF ST. BEDE'S. Bryson. net, $0.85.

KLONDIKE PICNIC, A. Donnelly. net, $0.85.
LAST LAP, THE. McGrath, S.J. net, $1.50.
LITTLE APOSTLE ON CRUTCHES. Delamare. net, $0.60.
LITTLE GIRL FROM BACK EAST. Roberts. net, $0.60.
LITTLE LADY OF THE HALL. Ryeman. net, $0.60.
LITTLE MARSHALLS AT THE LAKE. Nixon-Roulet. net, $0.85.
LITTLE MISSY. Waggaman. net, $0.60.
LOYAL BLUE AND ROYAL SCARLET. Taggart. net, $1.25.
LORD BOUNTIFUL. Finn, S.J. net, $1.00.
LUCKY BOB. Finn, S.J. net, $1.00.
MADCAP SET AT ST. ANNE'S. Brunowe. net, $0.60.
MAD KNIGHT, THE. Schaching. net, $0.60.
MAKING OF MORTLAKE. Copus, S.J. net, $0.85.
MAN FROM NOWHERE. Sadlier. net, $0.85.
MARKS OF THE BEAR CLAWS. Spalding, S.J. net, $1.00.
MARTHA JANE. Speckins. net, $1.50.
MARY ROSE AT BOARDING SCHOOL. Wirries. net, $1.00.
MARY ROSE KEEPS HOUSE. Wirries. net, $1.00.
MARY ROSE SOPHOMORE. Wirries. net, $1.00.
MARY TRACY'S FORTUNE. Sadlier. net, $0.60.
MILLY AVELING. Smith. net, $0.85.
MIRALDA. Johnson. net, $0.60.
MOSTLY BOYS. Finn, S.J. net, $1.00.
MYSTERIOUS DOORWAY. Sadlier. net, $0.60.
MYSTERY OF CLEVERLY. Barton. net, $0.85.
MYSTERY OF HORNBY HALL. Sadlier. net, $0.85.
NAN NOBODY. Waggaman. net, $0.60.
NED RIEDER. Wehs. net, $0.85.
NEW SCHOLAR AT ST. ANNE'S. Brunowe. net, $0.85.
OLD CHARLMONT'S SEED BED. Smith. net, $0.60.

OLD MILL ON THE WITHROSE. Spalding, S.J. net, $1.00.
ON THE OLD CAMPING GROUND. Mannix. net, $0.85.
ON THE RUN. Finn, S.J. net, $1.00.
ON THE SANDS OF CONEY. Boyton, S.J. net, $1.25.
PAMELA'S LEGACY. Taggart. net, $1.50.
PANCHO AND PANCHITA. Mannix. net, $0.60.
PAULINE ARCHER. Sadlier. net, $0.60.
PERCY WYNN. Finn, S.J. net, $1.00.
PERIL OF DIONYSIO. Mannix. net, $0.60.
PETRONILLA. Donnelly. net, $0.85.
PICKLE AND PEPPER. Dorsey. net, $1.25.
PILGRIM FROM IRELAND. Carnot. net, $0.60.
PLAYWATER PLOT, THE. Waggaman. net, $1.25.
POLLY DAY'S ISLAND. Roberts. net, $0.85.
POVERINA. Buckenham. net, $0.85.
QUEEN'S PAGE, THE. Hinkson. net, $0.60.
QUEEN'S PROMISE, THE. Waggaman. net, $1.25.
QUEST OF MARY SELWYN. Clementia. net, $1.50.
RACE FOR COPPER ISLAND. Spalding, S.J. net, $1.00.
REARDON RAH! Holland, S.J. net, $1.25.
RECRUIT TOMMY COLLINS. Bonesteel. net, $0.60.
ST. CUTHBERT'S. Copus, S.J. net, $0.85.
SANDY JOE. Waggaman. net, $1.25.
SEA-GULL'S ROCK. Sandeau. net, $0.60.
SEVEN LITTLE MARSHALLS. Nixon-Roulet. net, $0.60.
SHADOWS LIFTED. Copus, S.J. net, $0.85.
SHERIFF OF THE BEECH FORK. Spalding, S.J. net, $1.00.
SHIPMATES. Waggaman. net, $1.25.
SIGNALS FROM THE BAY TREE. Spalding, S.J. net, $1.00.
STRANDED ON LONG BAR. Spalding, S.J. net, $1.00.
STRONG ARM OF AVALON. Waggaman. net, $1.25.
SUGAR CAMP AND AFTER. Spalding, S.J. net, $1.00.
SUMMER AT WOODVILLE. Sadlier. net, $0.60.
SUNSHINE AND FRECKLES. Finn, S.J. net, $1.00.
TALISMAN, THE. Sadlier. net, $0.85.
TAMING OF POLLY. Dorsey. net, $1.25.
THAT FOOTBALL GAME. Finn, S.J. net, $1.00.
THAT OFFICE BOY. Finn, S.J. net, $1.00.
THREE GIRLS AND ESPECIALLY ONE. Taggart. net, $0.60.
TOLD IN THE TWILIGHT. Salome. net, $0.85.
TOM LOSELY: BOY. Copus, S.J. net, $0.85.
TOM PLAYFAIR. Finn, S.J. net, $1.00.
TOM'S LUCK-POT. Waggaman. net, $0.60.
TOORALLADDY. Walsh. net, $0.60.
TRANSPLANTING OF TESSIE. Waggaman. net, $1.25.
TREASURE OF NUGGET MOUNTAIN. Taggart. net, $0.85.
TWO LITTLE GIRLS. Mack. net, $0.60.
UNCLE FRANK'S MARY. Clementia. net, $1.50.
UPS AND DOWNS OF MARJORIE. Waggaman. net, $0.60.
VIOLIN MAKER. Smith. net, $0.60.
WHERE MONKEYS SWING. Boyton. net, $1.25.
WINNETOU, THE APACHE KNIGHT. Taggart. net, $0.85.
WHOOPEE! Boyton, S.J. net, $1.25.
YOUNG COLOR GUARD. Bonesteel. net, $0.60.

VII. NOVELS

ISABEL C. CLARKE'S GREAT NOVELS. Each, net, $2.00.
SELMA.
IT HAPPENED IN ROME.
VILLA BY THE SEA, THE.
CHILDREN OF THE SHADOW.
VIOLA HUDSON.
ANNA NUGENT.
CARINA.

AUTOGRAPH FICTION LIBRARY. Each, net, $1.50.
AVERAGE CABINS.
THE LIGHT ON THE LAGOON.
THE POTTER'S HOUSE.
TRESSIDER'S SISTER.
URSULA FINCH.
THE ELSTONES.
EUNICE.
LADY TRENT'S DAUGHTER.
CHILDREN OF EVE.
THE DEEP HEART.
WHOSE NAME IS LEGION.
FINE CLAY.
PRISONERS' YEARS.
THE REST HOUSE.
ONLY ANNE.
THE SECRET CITADEL.
BY THE BLUE RIVER.

ALBERTA: ADVENTURESS. L'Ermite. net, $2.00.
AVERAGE CABINS. Clarke. net, $1.50.
ANNA NUGENT. Clarke. net, $2.00.
BACK TO THE WORLD. Champol. net, $2.00.
BALLADS OF CHILDHOOD. Poems. Earls, S.J. net, $1.50.
BOND AND FREE. Connor. net, $0.85.
BOY Inez Specking. net, $1.25.
BUNNY'S HOUSE. Walker. net, $2.00.
BUT THY LOVE AND THY GRACE. Finn. net, $1.00.
BY THE BLUE RIVER. Clarke. net, $1.50.
CARINA. Clarke. net, $2.00.
CABLE, THE. Taggart. net, $2.00.
CARROLL 'DARE. Waggaman. net, $0.85.
CHILDREN OF THE SHADOW. Clarke. net, $2.00.
CONNOR'S DAUGHTER. Bertholds. net, $0.85.

CHILDREN OF EVE. Clarke. net, $1.50.
CONNOR D'ARCY'S STRUGGLES. Bertholds. net, $0.85.
DEEP HEART, THE. Clarke. net, $1.50.
DENYS THE DREAMER. Hinkson. net, $0.85.
DION AND THE SIBYLS. Keon. net, $0.85.
ELDER MISS AINSBOROUGH, THE. Taggart. net, $0.85.
ELSTONES, THE. Clarke. net, $1.50.
EUNICE. Clarke. net, $1.50.
FABIOLA. Wiseman. net, $0.85.
FABIOLA'S SISTERS. Clarke. net, $0.85.
FALSE GODS. Will Scarlet. net, $2.00.
FAUSTULA. Ayscough. net, $2.00.
FINE CLAY. Clarke. net, $1.50.
FOR BETTER FOR WORSE. Scott, S.J. net, $1.75.
FORGIVE AND FORGET. Lingen. net, $0.85.
GRAPES OF THORNS. Waggaman. net, $0.85.
HEIRESS OF CRONENSTEIN. Hahn-Hahn. net, $0.85.
HER BLIND FOLLY. Holt. net, $0.85.
HER JOURNEY'S END. Cooke. net, $0.85.
IDOLS; OR THE SECRET OF THE RUE CHAUSSE D'ANTIN. de Navery. net, $0.85.
IN GOD'S COUNTRY. Boyton. S.J. net, $2.00.
IN GOD'S GOOD TIME. Ross. net, $0.85.
IN SPITE OF ALL. Staniforth. net, $0.85.
IT HAPPENED IN ROME. Clarke. net, $2.00.
KELLY. Scott. S.J. net, $1.50.
KIND HEARTS AND CORONETS. Harrison. net, $0.85.
LADY TRENT'S DAUGHTER. Clarke. net, $1.50.
LIGHT OF HIS COUNTENANCE. Hart. net, $0.85.
LIGHT ON THE LAGOON, THE. Clarke. net, $1.50.
"LIKE UNTO A MERCHANT." Gray. net, $0.85.
LOVE OF BROTHERS. Hinkson. net, $0.85.

12

MARCELLA GRACE. Mulholland. net, $0.85.
MARIQUITA. Ayscough. net, $2.00.
MIRAGE. Specking. net, $1.50.
MISS ERIN. Francis. net, $0.85.
MISSY. Specking. net, $1.25.
MONK'S PARDON, THE. De Nerry. net, $0.85.
MY LADY BEATRICE. Cooke. net, $0.85.
NO HANDICAP. Taggart. net, $2.00.
NOT A JUDGMENT. Kzon. net, $1.65.
ONLY ANNE. Clarke. net, $1.50.
OTHER MISS LISLE. Martin. net, $0.85.
OUTLAW OF CAMARGUE. De Lamothe. net, $0.85.
PASSING SHADOWS. Yorke. net, $1.65.
PAT. Hineson. net, $0.85.
POTTER'S HOUSE, THE. Clarke. net, $1.50.
PRISONERS' YEARS. Clarke. net, $1.50.
PROPHET'S WIFE. Brown. net, $0.85.
REST HOUSE, THE. Clarke. net, $1.50.
ROSE OF THE WORLD. Martin. net, $0.85.
ROUND TABLE OF AMERICAN CATHOLIC NOVELISTS. net, $0.50.
ROUND TABLE OF FRENCH CATHOLIC NOVELISTS. net, $0.50.
ROUND TABLE OF IRISH AND ENGLISH CATHOLIC NOVELISTS. net, $0.50.
RUBY CROSS, THE. Wallace. net, $0.85.
RULER OF THE KINGDOM. Kzon. net, $1.65.
SECRET CITADEL, THE Clarke. net, $1.50.
SECRET OF THE GREEN VASE. Cooke. net, $0.85.
SELMA. Clarke. net, $2.00.
SHADOW OF EVERSLEIGH. Lansdowne. net, $0.85.
SO AS BY FIRE. Connor. net, $0.85.
SON OF SIRO, THE. Copus, S.J. net, $2.00.
TEMPEST OF THE HEART. Gray. net, $0.85.
TEST OF COURAGE. Ross. net, $0.85.
TRESSIDER'S SISTER. Clarke. net, $1.50.
TURN OF THE TIDE, THE. Gray. net, $0.85.
UNBIDDEN GUEST, THE. Cooke. net, $0.85.
UNDER THE CEDARS AND THE STARS. Canon Sheehan. net, $2.00.
URSULA FINCH. Clarke. net, $1.50.
VILLA BY THE SEA, THE. Clarke. net, $2.00.
VIOLA HUDSON. Clarke. net, $2.00.
WARGRAVE TRUST, THE Reid. net, $1.65.
WAR MOTHERS. Poems. Garesche, S.J. net, $0.60.
WAY THAT LED BEYOND, THE. Harrison. net, $0.85.
WHOSE NAME IS LEGION. Clarke. net, $1.50.

www.ingramcontent.com/pod-product-compliance
Lightning Source LLC
Chambersburg PA
CBHW020922230426
43666CB00008B/1537